SCHOLAR Study Guide

CfE Higher Economics
Unit 3: Global economic activity

Authored by:

Colin Spence (Culloden Academy)

Reviewed by:

Wilson Turkington (Edinburgh Academy)

Previously authored by:

Bill McFarlane

Colin Spence

Tommy Stewart

Heriot-Watt University

Edinburgh EH14 4AS, United Kingdom.

First published 2015 by Heriot-Watt University.

This edition published in 2015 by Heriot-Watt University SCHOLAR.

Copyright © 2015 SCHOLAR Forum.

Distributed by the SCHOLAR Forum.

SCHOLAR Study Guide Unit 3: CfE Higher Economics

1. CfE Higher Economics Course Code: C722 76

ISBN 978-1-909633-46-9

Print Production and fulfilment in UK by Print Trail www.printtrail.com

Acknowledgements

Thanks are due to the members of Heriot-Watt University's SCHOLAR team who planned and created these materials, and to the many colleagues who reviewed the content.

We would like to acknowledge the assistance of the education authorities, colleges, teachers and students who contributed to the SCHOLAR programme and who evaluated these materials.

Grateful acknowledgement is made for permission to use the following material in the SCHOLAR programme:

The Scottish Qualifications Authority for permission to use Past Papers assessments.

The Scottish Government for financial support.

The content of this Study Guide is aligned to the Scottish Qualifications Authority (SQA) curriculum.

Contents

Topic 1

Understanding global trade

Contents

Prerequisite knowledge

The topic builds on and expands the concept of trade studied in National 5 Economics. However, prior knowledge of this concept, although useful, is not essential.

Learning objectives

By the end of this topic you should be able to:

- *name the major UK exports;*
- *name the major UK imports;*
- *describe the reasons for global trade;*
- *explain the benefits of trade for consumers and companies;*
- *explain the advantages and disadvantages of global trade;*
- *explain the theory of absolute advantage;*
- *explain the theory of comparative advantage;*

- *explain trends in UK export and import patterns;*
- *name the UK's major trading partners;*
- *understand why it is more likely the UK will trade with some nations than others.*

1.1 UK imports

The following information on the origin and composition of UK **imports** comes from the government's '**Pink Book**'. The top 20 countries of origin of UK imports of goods in 2011 are shown below (UK imports of services are in brackets).

1.	Germany (4)	11.	Japan (5)
2.	China (23)	12.	Sweden (15)
3.	USA (1)	13.	Hong Kong (21)
4.	Netherlands (8)	14.	Switzerland (9)
5.	Norway (19)	15.	Russia (27)
6.	France (2)	16.	Poland (20)
7.	Belgium/Luxembourg (11/17*)	17.	Canada (16)
8.	Italy (6)	18.	Denmark (21)
9.	Ireland (7)	19.	India (10)
10.	Spain (3)	20.	Turkey (19)

The missing top 20 nations in the 'services' list are Australia (12), Singapore (13), Greece (14) and Portugal (18).

*Note that Belgium and Luxembourg are separated for services, but together for goods.

UK imports - EU countries

Q1: Select those countries which are in the EU, from the top 20 nations above.

. . . .

Go online

In summary, the most important sources for UK imports of goods are the European Union, the United States, China, Norway and Japan. The most important sources for UK imports of services are very similar. Note that China and Norway are significantly lower on the services list and India is fairly significant as a source of imports for services.

The higher positions of Spain, Greece, Portugal and Cyprus will reflect the importance of UK tourists to these countries.

1.1.1 UK imports (composition)

Compare the imports with the exports in the same categories in the section *1.2.1 UK exports (composition)* and you may spot the following:

- the UK is now a net importer of oil;
- far from being the nineteenth century "workshop of the world" we are now net importers of both semi-manufactured and finished goods;

- the latest figures for whisky exports can be accessed online - an article in January 2015 claimed this was the most significant sector in the category 'food and drink'. (Note that news articles are currently available from The Guardian and The Daily Telegraph websites without pay walls. The BBC is another useful source.)

The table below shows the composition of UK imports of goods in 2011 with the amount imported (shown in millions of pounds).

Trade in goods (imports)	Amount imported (in £millions)
Food, beverages and tobacco	36,069
Basic materials	11,928
Oil	49,490
Coal, gas and electricity	12,353
Semi-manufactured goods	196,494
Finished manufactured goods	187,701
Others	3,542

The table below shows the composition of UK imports of services in 2011 with the amount imported (shown in millions of pounds).

Trade in services (imports)	Amount imported (in £millions)
Transportation	19,951
Travel	31,830
Communications	4,704
Construction	1,065
Insurance	2,197
Financial	12,170
Computer and information	3,993
Royalties and license fees	6,654
Other business	30,246
Personal, cultural and recreational	640
Government	3,829

1.2 UK exports

The following information on the origin and composition of UK **exports** comes from the government's '**Pink Book**'. The top 20 countries of origin of UK exports of goods in 2011 are shown below (UK exports of services are in brackets).

1.	USA (1)	11.	India (21)
2.	Germany (2)	12.	Switzerland (6)
3.	Netherlands (3)	13.	Hong Kong (23)
4.	France (4)	14.	Russia (25)
5.	Ireland (5)	15.	United Arab Emirates (24)
6.	Belgium/Luxembourg (15/20)	16.	Canada (12)
7.	Italy (8)	17.	Japan (10)
8.	Spain (9)	18.	Australia (7)
9.	China (14)	19.	Poland (27)
10.	Sweden (13)	20.	Turkey (31)

The missing top 20 nations in the 'services' list in brackets are: Singapore (11), Denmark (16), The Channel Islands (17), Norway (18) and Saudi Arabia (19).

*Note that Belgium and Luxembourg are separated for services, but together for goods.

In summary, the most important destinations for UK exports of goods are the European Union and the United States. The most important destinations for UK exports of services are very similar.

1.2.1 UK exports (composition)

The table below shows the composition of UK exports of goods in 2011 with the amount exported (shown in millions of pounds).

Trade in goods (exports)	Amount exported (in £millions)
Food, beverages and tobacco	18,098
Basic materials	9,017
Oil	37,998
Coal, gas and electricity	4,724
Semi-manufactured goods	88,056
Finished manufactured goods	137,246
Others	3,848

The table below shows the composition of UK exports of services in 2011 with the amount exported (shown in millions of pounds).

Trade in services (exports)	Amount exported (in £millions)
Transportation	23,120
Travel	21,888
Communications	6,465
Construction	1,653
Insurance	10,210
Financial	50,833
Computer and information	9,167
Royalties and license fees	8,848
Other business	56,126
Personal, cultural and recreational	2,877
Government	2,472

1.2.2   UK trade by category

The table below gives a breakdown of UK exports and imports of goods by category in 2001 and a comparison with UK exports and imports of goods in 2011 to see if we can establish trends.

For simplification only a selection of the total number of categories is used in the table below. To understand this table you will need to be aware that the year 2009 is the base year and therefore awarded a volume index of 100 in every case. All the numbers relate to the volume (quantity) of goods, rather than the value.

Category	Exports			Imports		
	2001	2009	2011	2001	2009	2011
Crude oil	191	100	74	83	100	108
Oil products	62	100	97	107	100	86
Motor cars	74	100	165	104	100	122
Finished manufactured goods	104	100	123	91	100	114
Food, beverages and tobacco	83	100	113	78	100	102

Trade in goods (volume) by category

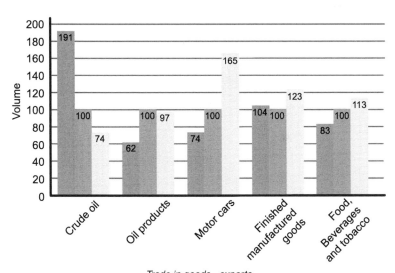

Trade in goods - exports

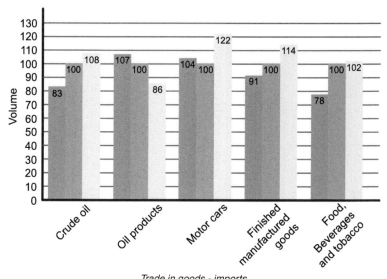

Trade in goods - imports

Analyse these figures to answer the following statements as true or false.

Go online

UK trade by category

Q2: Exports of crude oil have reduced between 2001 and 2011.

a) True
b) False

....

Q3: Imports of total finished manufactured goods have reduced between 2001 and 2011.

a) True
b) False

....

Q4: Between 2009 and 2011, exports of cars grew faster than import of cars.

a) True
b) False

....

Q5: The UK's exports of food, beverages and tobacco have remained largely flat over the period 2001 to 2011.

a) True
b) False

....

Q6: Exports of total finished manufactured goods have declined over the decade.

a) True
b) False

....

Note that given the big changes in the value of a barrel of oil over these 10 years, that a fall in the *volume* of oil exports should not be taken to automatically mean a fall in the *value* of oil exports.

....

1.3 The advantages of trade

The theories of absolute and comparative advantage highlight one significant gain from trade. The world will produce more output from the same resource inputs. Other gains from trade can be categorised as gains for consumers or gains for producers.

The gains for consumers are:

- *variety* - new products from around the world;
- *choice* - greater variety of brands to select from;
- *price* - lower prices because of the increased competition;
- *quality* - competition encourages quality improvements and innovation.

The gains for producers are:

- *larger market* - opportunities for **economies of scale** increase with the greater number of customers;
- **diversification** - more than one market gives the benefits of diversification. Companies facing a recession at home will still hope to sell in export markets and vice versa;
- **multinational activity** - firms can produce at lowest cost locations, to increase efficiency and cut prices;
- *raw materials and components* - can be sourced from the cheapest locations around the world.

The advantages of trade

Q7: Giving three reasons, explain why countries engage in trade.

Go online   *(6 marks)*

....

Impact of international trade

Trade is likely to have an impact on UK consumers in the five areas in the questions

Go online   below. In each case state whether trade is likely to decrease or increase.

Q8: Choice

a) Increase
b) Decrease

....

Q9: Competition

a) Increase
b) Decrease

....

Q10: Prices

a) Increase
b) Decrease

....

Q11: Quality

a) Increase
b) Decrease

....

Q12: Standard of living

a) Increase
b) Decrease

....

1.4   The disadvantages of trade

The disadvantages of trade are:

- workers (especially less-skilled workers) may lose their jobs to lower-wage economies as firms move production overseas;

- local firms may go out of business in the face of efficient competition from low-cost locations. The resulting unemployment may be concentrated in one region. Workers will need to be flexible and retrain, or move to a new location;

- the movement of goods around the planet will add to pollution;

- reliance on imports for some products may impinge on national security. For example, a dependence on imported armaments may be a weakness in time of conflict.

1.5 Global specialisation

The gains from international trade are vast. The rapid expansion of world output and the accompanying increase in standards of living stem in part from the growth of international trade. Specialisation by countries is a similar concept to specialisation by workers. The economies of scale associated with all forms of specialisation are a powerful engine of economic growth.

Globalisation is the term coined for the rapid expansion of trade in the last few decades. It refers to the increasingly inter-connected world economy. Developments such as the internet and modern communications have been factors. They have assisted the move to internationally recognised brands, and the standardisation of products. It also stems from technological developments such as "containerisation" which reduces the cost of transport. Multi-national firms have moved their production facilities to new locations as they seek ever lower costs of production.

Trade creates synergies. A synergy describes a situation where the sum is greater than the parts. The gains from trade outnumber any disadvantages. Politicians recognise the gains from trade and devote much energy to creating free trade areas such as the European Union. Trade increases economic growth and the resulting rise in **standards of living** assists politicians in their re-election.

Globalisation

Q13: Complete the paragraph below by inserting the correct words from the following list:

Go online

- brand;
- containerisation;
- internet;
- locations;
- specialisation;
- synergies;
- trade;
- workers.

Globalisation describes the rapid expansion of international .... Some developments that have contributed are the reduction in the costs of transporting goods through the development of .... and the increasing ease of modern communications using the .... These developments have led to multi-national firms reducing costs by finding new .... for production plants and the increasing prevalence of internationally recognised .... names.

....

1.6   Absolute advantage

The **theory of absolute advantage** shows that trade has the potential to increase the efficiency with which the world's scarce resources are used. By increasing efficiency, trade can increase world output from the same amount of inputs. Any increase in world output contributes to reducing poverty on the planet, providing the benefits are distributed in a way that reaches the poorest.

To create our example of absolute advantage we must simplify the world's complex trading patterns. Assume that:

- there are only two nations;
- and there are only two products.

To make the example straightforward, we need to select two very diverse countries: Australia and Belize. We also need to select two diverse products as the only two products in our world: aircraft and bananas.

The selection of two countries and products with the initials *a* and *b* will assist you in remembering this example is about *ab*solute advantage.

Now we need to compare two positions, before trade and after trade, to find out if trade has benefits.

Before-trade output

Firstly, before trade, when both nations have to produce both goods for themselves. We assume that both countries have 100 units of factors of production. They have to produce both items so they each will use 50 factors to produce bananas and 50 factors to produce aircraft.

Australia is efficient at producing aircraft, but less so at producing bananas. In Australia, one factor of production will produce one aircraft. However, they find producing bananas more difficult and five factors of production are required for every ton of bananas.

Meantime, in Belize, bananas grow on trees and only one factor of production is needed to produce one ton of bananas. Producing aircraft in Belize would be expensive and difficult so it requires two factors of production to produce an aircraft.

The factors of production required for one unit of each output in each country are summarised in the efficiency table below. This shows the efficiency of each country at producing each product.

Country	Aircraft	Bananas (tons)
Australia	1	5
Belize	2	1

Efficiency table

We can use this table to work out how many of each product will be produced if no trade is taking place. Countries (with 100 factors each) use 50 factors for the production of each product.

Country	Aircraft	Bananas (tons)
Australia	50	10*
Belize	25	50
Total output (before trade)	75	60

Before-trade output

To ensure you understand how the figures above were calculated, have a close look at one of the figures. Our example* can be Australia producing 10 tons of bananas.

This is worked out as follows: Australia has 100 factor inputs, but because there is no trade and it also needs aircraft, we only allocate 50 (half) of the factor inputs to producing bananas. As Australia (see the efficiency table above) needs 5 factor inputs to produce 1 ton of bananas, then with its 50 factors it can only produce 10 tons of bananas. The other figures above are calculated in a similar way with reference to the efficiency table.

Finally, by adding the figures together we can see that total output before trade is 75 aircraft and 60 tons of bananas.

After-trade output

Next we allow trade between these nations. The inefficient producers are undercut by imports. It is no longer profitable for Australia to grow bananas or for Belize to make aircraft. If these products are produced in inefficient locations then the opportunity cost is high. Both countries specialise in what they are best at. All 100 factors are devoted to one product. The after-trade output follows:

Country	Aircraft	Bananas (tons)
Australia	100	0
Belize	0	100
Total output (after trade)	100	100

After-trade output

By specialising and trading, total output has risen by 25 aircraft (100 after trade less 75 before trade) and 40 tons of bananas (100 after less 60 before).

There was no increase in factor inputs. Factors of production (scarce resources) have merely been more efficiently used.

Transport costs

We have ignored transport costs - pretending they don't exist. The gains from international trade are so big that even after resources are used transporting products around the globe, there is still a gain. There are plentiful examples of how transport costs can be overcome. Fresh flowers flown in from Kenya to the UK and wine from New Zealand are two such examples. Clear evidence that even in the face of transportation costs from halfway round the globe, trade prospers and products can remain competitive.

Go online

Before-trade and after-trade output (absolute advantage)

The table below shows the output of two nations before trade. They must divide their factors of production equally between the manufacture of two goods.

Country	Cars	Vegetables
Urbania	50	20
Ruritania	40	60

Q14: What is the before-trade world output of cars?

. . . .

Q15: What is the before-trade world output of vegetables?

. . . .

Q16: What will be the after-trade world output of cars?

. . . .

Q17: What will be the after-trade world output of vegetables?

. . . .

Q18: Has world output increased as a result of trade?

a) Yes

b) No

....

1.7 Comparative advantage

The **theory of comparative advantage** refers to this situation - one nation has an efficiency advantage in making both products. We will test what happens if the advanced nation specialises in the product that it has the greatest efficiency advantage producing. This means we have to compare the efficiency advantages to find out which product the advanced nation has the greatest comparative advantage making.

To create our example we must again make assumptions to simplify the world's complex trading patterns. We therefore assume that:

- there are only two nations;

- there are only two products;

- transport costs are negligible;

- our inputs are homogeneous factors of production;

- these factors are flexible in changing use as required.

We need to select two goods to produce as the only two products in our world: cars and oranges. The choice of products beginning with *c* and *o* will help you associate this example with *co*mparative advantage.

Our two countries can be the USA and Mexico. We can realistically view the USA as the more advanced economy in this example.

Now we need to compare two positions, before trade and after trade, to find out if trade is still beneficial to both countries.

Before-trade output

Firstly, before trade, when both nations have to produce both goods for themselves. We assume that both countries have 100 units of factors of production. Because they have to produce both products, they each will use 50 factors to produce cars and 50 factors to produce oranges.

The USA has an absolute advantage in producing *both* cars and oranges. This can be shown in the efficiency table below, showing factors of production required for one unit of each output in each country.

Country	Cars	Oranges (tons)
USA	1	2
Mexico	2	5

Efficiency table

We can use this table to work out how many of each product will be produced if no trade is taking place. Countries (with 100 factors each) then have to use 50 factors for the production of each product.

Country	Cars	Oranges (tons)
USA	50	25*
Mexico	25	10
Total output (before trade)	75	35

Before-trade output

To ensure you understand how the figures above were calculated, have a close look at one of the figures. Our example* can be the USA producing 25 tons of oranges.

This is worked out as follows: the USA has 100 factor inputs, but because there is no trade and it needs to produce both cars and oranges, we only allocate half (50) of the factor inputs to producing oranges. As the USA (see the efficiency table above) needs two factor inputs to produce one ton of oranges, then with its 50 factors it can produces 25 tons of oranges. The other figures above are calculated in a similar way with reference to the efficiency table.

Finally, by adding the figures together we can see that total output before trade is 75 cars and 35 tons of oranges.

Logically you may at first glance expect there to be no gain for the USA from trading with a less efficient nation. As we will shortly see, the theory of comparative advantage proves that trade will still lead to a more effective use of scarce resource inputs. Even when one nation is more efficient in making both products it will allow an increase in total world output from the same quantity of inputs.

After-trade output (temporary)

Next we allow trade between these nations. First we have to recognise that the USA is two times as efficient at producing cars as Mexico. The USA produces 50 cars with 50 inputs of factors of production. In the case of oranges the USA is 2.5 times as efficient. It produces 25 tons of oranges with 50 inputs whereas Mexico produces 10 tons with 50 inputs. Look again at the efficiency table above to confirm this.

As a temporary step on the way to proving comparative advantage, we need to allow the USA to produce only that product in which it has the greatest comparative advantage. In this example that will be oranges. This is because it is 2.5 times as efficient at producing oranges and only 2 times as efficient at producing cars. Therefore Mexico has the least comparative disadvantage in producing cars. The after-trade output will temporarily look like this:

Country	Cars	Oranges (tons)
USA	0	50
Mexico	50	0
Total output	50	50

After-trade output (temporary)

You will notice that so far we are unable to confirm that world output has increased. We have more oranges and fewer cars.

After-trade output (amended)

One adjustment must be made to confirm that world output can increase. We allow the efficient nation to produce just enough cars to take us back to the original before-trade world output of 75 cars. We reduce their oranges production appropriately to reflect that some factors have been diverted back into car production.

Now with the USA making up the shortfall in cars, we obtain the following amended after-trade output.

Country	Cars	Oranges (tons)
USA	25	37.5
Mexico	50	0
Total output after trade	75	37.5

After-trade output (amended)

Now we have proved that world output has increased. We have the same number of cars and more oranges than we had before trade. Therefore the theory of comparative advantage proves that even when trade occurs between advanced economies and less efficient economies, it is effective in raising world output and improving the use of scarce resources.

Before-trade and after-trade output (comparative advantage)

Go online

This table shows the output of two nations before trade. They must divide their factors of production equally between the manufacture of two goods. Answer the questions that follow the table.

Country	Cars	Vegetables
Urbania	50	40
Ruritania	10	20

Q19: Both nations will benefit from specialisation and trade.

a) True
b) False

....

Q20: Ruritania has a comparative advantage in producing cars.

a) True
b) False

....

Q21: Urbania enjoys an absolute advantage in producing both cars and vegetables.

a) True
b) False

....

Q22: This is an example that can illustrate the theory of comparative advantage.

a) True
b) False

....

Q23: After trade, Ruritania will specialise in producing vegetables.

a) True
b) False

....

David Ricardo

The original explanation of comparative advantage (1817) is attributed to David Ricardo, the classical economist, in his book 'On the Principles of Political Economy and Taxation'. His example used Portugal and England, with the two products of cloth and wine.

Use the internet to find and read the original example from 200 years ago.

....

1.8   Trends in UK imports and exports

Let us now compare UK exports of goods in 2006 with UK exports of goods in 2012 to
see if we can establish trends. To simplify we will select only five nations: United
States, Germany, China, India and Japan. Germany's inclusion, the one example
selected from the EU, is as a representative of the overall significance of EU nations.

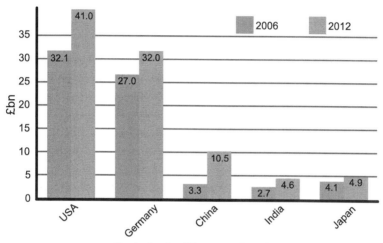

Graph showing UK exports of goods

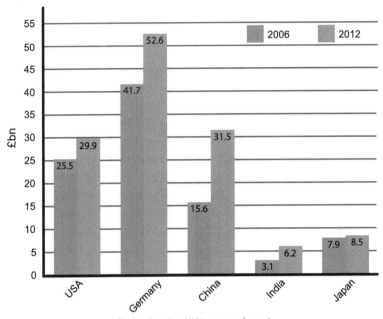

Graph showing UK imports of goods

Analysing the figures in the above graphs it is possible to come to the following conclusions about the geographic trends of UK trade:

- Despite closer links with the EU, the USA remains a major trading partner. In 2012 we had a surplus with the USA in trade in goods;

- Germany is another very significant trading partner, and it can be inferred that trade with other EU nations has also grown substantially. In the case of Germany we have a continuing deficit in trade in goods;

- The value of imports of goods from China has risen substantially in six years. Exports to China are also growing;

- Trade in goods with India is growing, but trade in goods with Japan has been quite flat over the decade. Japan remains a more significant trading partner than India, but perhaps not for much longer.

Trade surplus or deficit

Go online

Q24: Looking at the 2012 figures in the above five-nation graphs. Work out where the UK has a trade surplus in goods (exports more than imports) and where the UK has a trade deficit in goods (imports more than it exports).

Complete the table below, indicating whether the country has a trade surplus or deficit by entering Yes in the correct column.

Trade in goods (2006)	Trade surplus	Trade deficit
USA		
Germany		
China		
India		
Japan		

....

1.9 Patterns and reasons for trends in trade

When analysing the trade of the UK, the application of some everyday logic is a good way to start. Even without any specialised knowledge of Economics there is a good chance that you would select the correct options in the following activity.

Patterns and reasons for trends in trade

Select from the following pairs of statements the ones that you believe to be true.

Go online

Q25: It is easiest and cheapest to trade with .... nations.

a) neighbouring
b) distant

....

Q26: We can expect to sell more exports to nations with .... prosperous consumers.

a) less
b) more

....

Q27: We are likely to sell more exports to nations with .... populations.

a) large
b) small

....

Q28: We are .... likely to trade with fellow members of a free trade area.

a) more
b) less

....

The factors making large-scale trade with another nation probable are:

- **Geographic closeness** - transport costs have to be added to any product that is traded, and these will be less if the distance involved is less. This will allow traded products to sell at competitive prices in nearby export markets.

  If you are to sell goods successfully in a distant market, you will need to be very efficient producers so that even after long-distance transport costs, your goods are still price-competitive. Distant markets may be distant in a socio-cultural way as well as geographically and consumers may have very different tastes and expectations;

- **Prosperous consumers** - the higher the standard of living of the consumers, the more they will buy of all products (including your **exports**). Internationally traded goods are often luxury goods. For example, if you hope to sell cars in a foreign country, then high-income consumers are needed;

- **Large population** - the greater the number of potential consumers of your exports, the more likely you are to find a large market for your exports. The **European Union** has over 500 million consumers making it a very significant for UK trade. Similarly the United States is a very large and prosperous market for UK goods;

- **Free trade** - as yet you have not had free trade explained to you, but it sounds like a positive term and it is. Trade is more likely to occur if no obstacles such as taxes are put in the way. The European Union is a free trade area of 28 countries (in 2014) and over 500 million consumers.

Go online

Trading nations

Look at the data in the table below then consider how the following four nations "tick the boxes" for our factors making large-scale trade probable.

Nation	Near UK	Rich	Populated	EU member
Ireland	√	√	x	√
Japan	x	√	√	x
Germany	√	√	√	√
Morocco	x	x	x	x

Q29: Which of the above four nations would you expect the UK to export *most* to?

a) Ireland
b) Japan
c) Germany
d) Morocco

. . . .

Q30: Which of the above four nations would you expect the UK to export *least* to?

a) Ireland
b) Japan
c) Germany
d) Morocco

....

From this approach you can see that Germany will be an important market for the UK's exports. It offers over 80 million affluent consumers just across the North Sea and has no trade barriers to UK goods.

Morocco is clearly unlikely to import much from the UK. Between them in importance will lie Japan and Ireland. We would have to guess if Japan's 127 million consumers compared to Ireland's 4.3 million will compensate for Japan's distance and non-membership of the EU.

Trading nations - Japan and Ireland

Q31: Considering only Japan and Ireland, which would you expect the UK to export more to?

Go online

a) Ireland
b) Japan

....

A little bit of research on the internet will check if our predictions are correct. On the internet it is possible to access the UK's trade figures in the UK Government's Pink Book. This provides the following data, in the graph below, for 2012.

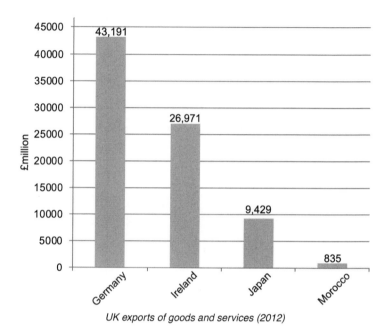

UK exports of goods and services (2012)

The results show the importance of nearness and membership of a free trade area. Ireland has significance for our exports out of proportion to its small population.

1.10 Summary

Summary

You should now know that:

- the UK's most significant trading partners are the European Union and the USA;

- our major exports of goods include finished manufactured goods, semi-manufactured goods, crude oil and oil products, and food, beverages and tobacco. We import more goods in the same categories and have a trade in goods deficit;

- in services, the UK is a major exporter of financial services. Transportation and travel feature highly in the value of UK imported services. The UK has a trade in services surplus;

- trade involves specialisation among nations;

- trade increases world output;

- trade increases competition resulting in greater variety, quality and innovation;

- increased competition also reduces prices;

- increased standards of living result as falling prices allow consumers to buy more with their incomes;

- trade will cause some workers to lose their jobs to foreign competition;

- trade with emerging economies such as China is increasing;

- trade with the EU and the USA remains of great significance;

- trade patterns reflect the geographic closeness, prosperity and population of partner nations, along with the absence/level of trade barriers.

1.11   End of topic test

End of Topic 1 test

Q32: Describe the main trends in UK trade.

Go online

(12 marks)

....

Q33: Which of the following nations specialises in financial services because of an educated workforce?

a) Canada
b) China
c) Israel
d) Italy
e) United Kingdom
f) Zambia

....

Q34: Which of the following nations specialises in wine production because of a suitable climate and soil?

a) Canada
b) China
c) Israel
d) Italy
e) United Kingdom
f) Zambia

....

Q35: Which of the following nations specialises in basic manufactured goods because of low labour costs?

a) Canada
b) China
c) Israel
d) Italy
e) United Kingdom
f) Zambia

....

Q36: Which of the following nations specialises in wheat production on abundant land?

a) Canada
b) China
c) Israel
d) Italy
e) United Kingdom
f) Zambia

....

Q37: Which of the following nations specialises in oranges because of climate?

a) Canada
b) China
c) Israel
d) Italy
e) United Kingdom
f) Zambia

. . . .

Q38: Which of the following nations specialises in copper production by mining a natural resource?

a) Canada
b) China
c) Israel
d) Italy
e) United Kingdom
f) Zambia

. . . .

Q39: Complete the paragraph below by inserting the correct words from the following list:

- bananas;
- choice;
- competition;
- living;
- prices;
- quality;
- standard.

As a result of trade, consumers will have more .... , for example, ... , that cannot be easily grown in the UK. Companies will face increased .... and as a result will have to increase .... and reduce .... to stay in business. This will mean that consumers will have a higher .... of ....

. . . .

Q40: Explain the theories of absolute and comparative advantage. *(SQA 2007)*

(8 marks)

. . . .

Topic 2

Multinationals

Contents

Prerequisite knowledge

This topic assumes no previous knowledge and is intended to be accessible for those studying Economics for the first time. However, if you have already completed National 5 Grade Economics you will be familiar with some of the concepts outlined.

Learning objectives

By the end of this topic you should be able to:

- *define the term 'multinational' and name an example;*

- *explain the factors that affect the location of a multinational;*

- *describe the effects of a multinational on the home and host countries.*

2.1   Defining multinational

A **multinational** is a company that is based in one country, but also has production or service facilities in other countries. It should not be confused with companies that merely export from their home base.

Most of the world's largest companies are multinationals, for example Ford, Nestle and BP. You can probably name some other examples off the top of your head.

The countries in which BP operates

Q1:   Go on to the BP website and compile a list of all the countries in which it operates.

....

2.2   Location factors

The location factors for multinationals, outlined below, are not very different from the location factors for any firm:

- **Costs of production** - Minimising costs of production is vital. To reduce costs, companies find locations where wages are lower and/or raw materials are cheaper. Transport and distribution costs to major markets cannot be overlooked and will come into the final decision.

  An additional factor may be the existence of tariffs or other trade barriers between nations, which could greatly restrict the choice of location.

- **Infrastructure** - This is a broad term which we can divide into three components:

  - *Transport* - Are the road, rail, sea and air links sufficient to allow the firm to operate efficiently and without unpredictable delays in getting goods to the market?

  - *Technology* - Does the country have access to the latest information and communications systems and will these systems function adequately?

  - *Institutional* - Is there a framework of business and contract law that facilitates business?

- **Markets** - This is a major factor. Developing local markets is often crucial to success, and multinationals may withdraw from markets where they cannot reach a suitable level of customer demand and are consequently unable to deliver the economies of scale that lead to profit.

- **Risk** - There are political and economic risks to consider. What are the chances of a violent revolution? Will the exchange rate of the currency move against you? Could there be an epidemic or a natural disaster such as a flood?

Go online

Location factors

Select the correct location factor group for the following location factors.

Q2: Good harbour facilities

a) Cost factors
b) Infrastructure concerns
c) Risk factors

. . . .

Q3: Hyperinflation

a) Cost factors
b) Infrastructure concerns
c) Risk factors

. . . .

Q4: Mobile phone communications

a) Cost factors
b) Infrastructure concerns
c) Risk factors

. . . .

Q5: Raw materials are cheaper

a) Cost factors
b) Infrastructure concerns
c) Risk factors

. . . .

Q6: Rebels in the hills

a) Cost factors
b) Infrastructure concerns
c) Risk factors

. . . .

Q7: Wages are lower

a) Cost factors
b) Infrastructure concerns
c) Risk factors

. . . .

2.3   The effects on the host country

Some of the effects on the host country in which a multinational operates include:

- creating employment, and this has a positive multiplier effect on the economy;
- training of workers;
- largely repatriating profits to the home nation, so profits are not always reinvested locally. This money leaves the host's circular flow as a leakage;
- improving standards by offering better working conditions than local firms;
- undercutting local firms' prices which may put them out of business;
- introducing modern technology and management methods;
- potentially causing pollution and long-term environmental damage;
- increasing exports, improving the balance of payments, and injecting money into the country's circular flow;
- delivering only low-skilled jobs, retaining top jobs in management and research at the home base;
- potentially may be footloose with little loyalty, and move on in a few years to a cheaper location;
- exploiting workers by taking advantage of weak labour laws.

The effects on the host country

Go online

Q8:   Separate the following effects on the host country into the positive or negative column in the table below:

- creates employment;
- improves working conditions;
- increases exports;
- introduces modern technology;
- may cause pollution;
- may switch location;
- only provides low skill jobs;
- profits often repatriated;
- trains workers;
- undercuts local firms' prices.

Positive	Negative

. . . .

2.4   The effects on the home country

Some of the effects on the home country in which a multinational operates include:

- jobs being lost overseas, with a negative multiplier effect;
- **deindustrialisation**, and loss of skills in the workforce;
- profits are often repatriated and contribute to investment in the home country;
- home-based firms continue to compete on world markets and survive (or even thrive);
- fewer exports and negative impact on balance of trade.

The effects on the home country

Go online

Q9:   Separate the following effects on the home country into the positive or negative column in the table below:

- deindustrialisation;
- fewer exports;
- jobs are lost overseas;
- profits repatriated;
- survival of home-based firm.

Positive	Negative

. . . .

2.5 Summary

Summary

You should now be able to:

- define the term 'multinational';
- describe location factors that multinationals must consider;
- describe effects on the home country;
- describe effects on the host country.

2.6   End   pic test

End of Topic 2 test

Q10: One example of a UK-based multinational would be:

Go online

a) Ford
b) Tata
c) Nestle
d) First Group

. . . .

Q11: A multinational company must:

a) export goods or services.
b) produce in more than one country.
c) Both of the above.
d) Neither of the above.

. . . .

Q12: One negative outcome for the host country of a multinational is:

a) the repatriation of profits.
b) the creation of low skilled jobs.
c) the introduction of modern technology.
d) increasing exports.

. . . .

Q13: One positive outcome for the home country of a multinational is:

a) deindustrialisation.
b) the repatriation of profits.
c) the creation of low skilled jobs.
d) increasing exports.

. . . .

Q14: One risk factor for multinationals to consider is:

a) training required for workers.
b) poor communications.
c) political instability.
d) poor transport infrastructure.

. . . .

Q15: Describe the factors that a multinational firm must consider before taking the decision to locate overseas.
(6 marks)

. . . .

Topic 3

Exchange rates

Contents

Prerequisite knowledge

This topic assumes no previous knowledge and is intended to be accessible for those studying Economics for the first time. However, if you have already completed National 5 Grade Economics you will be familiar with some of the concepts outlined.

Learning objectives

By the end of this topic you should be able to:

- *define the meaning of the term "exchange rate" and name several world currencies;*

- *explain why a currency is demanded or supplied;*

- *understand the effect of high and low exchange rates on individuals, firms and the current account;*

- *compare the advantages and disadvantages of fixed and floating exchange rates;*

- *describe the trends in the value of the £ over the last decade.*

3.1   Exchange rates

An **exchange rate** is the rate at which one currency can be converted into another. It is the value of one currency priced in a different currency.

Here are some exchange rates for currencies equal to 1 British pound sterling at the time this item was composed:

- 1.29 **Euros**;
- 1.52 US Dollars;
- 177.62 Japanese Yen;
- 1.55 Swiss Francs;
- 3.49 Turkish Lira;
- 94.36 Indian Rupees;
- 5.53 Polish Zloty;
- 9.40 Chinese Yuan.

An exchange rate is determined by market conditions. The market is called the foreign exchange market, sometimes abbreviated to **FOREX**. In this market, demand and supply interact to create the market price for a currency.

The fundamental reason why a currency has to be changed into another currency is to enable international transactions. However, the currency transactions required for trade to take place are now dwarfed by other market activity. Speculators buy and sell currencies as they see an opportunity to profit. Central banks, such as The Bank of England, intervene in foreign currency markets to influence the market price and enact a government's foreign exchange policy. Multi-national companies attempt to profit (or at least not lose) by their trading activity on the currency markets.

Current exchange rates

Research the current exchange rates for the eight currencies above.

There are many sites which will do this for you. One possibility is to go to the BBC website and follow the trail: news > business > market data > currencies. Another possibility is using a search engine. For example, using Google search for the term 'exchange rate pound' displays a currency converter at the top of the search results. A drop down menu of currencies allows you to compare the current value of the pound sterling with all the world's currencies.

Present your answers in a table using Word or Excel if possible. You can then look back in a week's time to see what the changes are. The actual exchange rates will vary from minute to minute, so there is no definitive solution to this activity, but you should compare and discuss your answers with a classmate.

....

3.2 The demand for sterling

The demand for sterling comes from the purchase of UK exports by foreign consumers and companies. The consumers pay in local currency and are unaware of their involvement, but somewhere down the supply chain an importer will need to convert the local cash into pounds because the UK producer expects to be paid in pounds. The foreign currency is presented (supplied) by the importer's bank to the foreign exchange market and pounds are demanded.

It follows that export success helps to drive the value of a country's currency upwards, because it increases demand for that currency. Apart from purchases of UK goods and services by foreign consumers and companies, foreign firms will need to obtain pounds if they are investing in the UK.

When the demand for pounds is higher than the supply, then the exchange rate of the pound will rise. This effect can be illustrated on the demand diagram below.

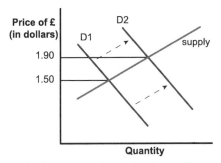

The market for currency: increasing demand for pounds

In the above diagram the demand for pounds increases from D1 to D2, shown by a rightwards movement of the demand line. The value of the pound increases and one pound is now able to buy $1.90 compared to $1.50 previously.

'**Hot money**' flows are placed in pounds whenever attractive interest rates are available in the UK. 'Hot money' describes liquid funds that can be switched to another currency at short notice. Increases in UK interest rates can lead to an increased demand for pounds, because of the improved returns available in UK banks. Therefore, increases in UK interest rates relative to the interest rates available elsewhere, will increase demand for pounds and take the value of the pound upwards.

Professionals operating in markets make money when they predict the next move by a market. Often when a change in interest rates happens, the market experts have already altered the currency value in the preceding days. The currency makes little further move and the markets are said to have discounted the interest rate change in advance. Expectations impact on the market as well as actual events.

Go online

Demand for currency

Select the option *increase* or *decrease* in the questions below to indicate whether or not the following scenarios would cause the demand for the pound to increase or decrease (other things being equal).

Q1: Expectation that the Bank of England is about to raise interest rates.

a) Increase
b) Decrease

....

Q2: The European Central Bank puts up the euro interest rate.

a) Increase
b) Decrease

....

Q3: Record levels of foreign investment in the UK.

a) Increase
b) Decrease

....

Q4: The US Federal Reserve puts down its dollar interest rate.

a) Increase
b) Decrease

....

3.3   The supply of sterling

As an effective student you should know that the reasons that cause an increase in the supply of a currency are largely the reverse of the factors listed as causing the demand for a currency.

UK consumers and companies purchasing imports will supply pounds to the foreign exchange market for conversion into the currency they require. UK companies investing overseas will do the same. Speculators can become involved in selling currencies and the Bank of England may also supply pounds to the market if it prefers the pound not to rise in value. Hot money can leave the UK as quickly as it arrives with one phone call or a tap on a computer.

When the supply of pounds is greater than demand then the exchange rate of the pound will fall. This effect can be illustrated on the supply diagram below.

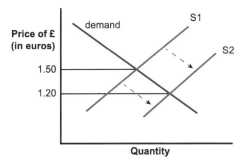

The market for currency: increasing supply of pounds

In the above diagram the supply of pounds increases from S1 to S2, shown by a rightwards movement of the supply line. The value of the pound decreases and it is now able to buy €1.20 compared to €1.50 previously.

The supply of currency

Select the appropriate words from the alternatives offered to reverse the section on demand for sterling. In the following three questions your aim is to make up correct sentences about the **supply** of pounds (sterling).

Go online

Q5: The (demand for/supply of) sterling comes from the purchase of UK (exports/imports) by (foreign/UK) consumers and companies.

....

Q6: It follows that (import penetration/export success) helps to drive the value of a country's currency (downwards/upwards), because it increases (demand for/supply of) that currency.

....

Q7: 'Hot money' flows are (placed in/taken out) of pounds whenever attractive interest rates are available (in the UK/outside the UK). (Increases/Decreases) in UK interest rates can lead to an (increased demand for/increased supply of) pounds, because of the (diminished/improved) returns available in UK banks.

....

3.4 The effect of a rising exchange rate on the economy

Exchange rates cause changes in other economic variables. We will now look closely at the effect a changing exchange rate can have on the levels of exports and imports, the inflation rate, economic growth and the level of employment.

When the pound increases, the price of UK exports in foreign markets will rise.

Example : Jaguar

Problem:

Let us consider a Jaguar car selling for £40,000.

At first the exchange rate is £1 = €1.25.

To allow Jaguar to receive the price of £40,000, the car will be priced at €50,000 in the eurozone (e.g. Germany). This is arithmetic: 40,000 × 1.25 converts the pounds into euros.

Next, the exchange rate of the pound increases to £1 = €1.50. Each pound will buy more euros than it used to, so this is described as the pound increasing in value.

Solution:

To allow Jaguar to receive the price of £40,000, the car will be now priced at €60,000 in the eurozone (e.g. Germany). To convert the pounds into euros we now multiply £40,000 × 1.5.

....

Therefore, we can conclude that a rise in the value of the pound is bad news for UK exporters such as Jaguar. To continue receiving £40,000 and maintain the profit margin on each car they will need to increase their eurozone price by 20%, exactly the percentage that the pound has risen by against the euro in our example. Meantime makers such as BMW and Mercedes are able to hold their prices, and thus Jaguar are at a competitive disadvantage.

It is feasible that companies who have invested heavily in acquiring market share or have a franchised dealer network may choose to take a cut in profits or even make a loss in the short term rather than see market share fall and their hard work undone. They cannot adopt this position for long.

Improving productivity can also offset price rises abroad but that would be a gradual process and could not compensate for a rapid increase in an exchange rate. Unless the exchange rate rise is temporary the price competitiveness of UK exports is bound to deteriorate. The volume of UK exports will therefore decrease.

By reversing the process described above, imports into the UK become cheaper. Our example, Jaguar, will be hit again. This time it will be under pressure in its UK home market because BMW and Mercedes will be able to reduce their price in pounds. The volume of UK imports will increase when the exchange rate of the pound rises.

Go online

The effect of a rising exchange rate on the economy

Q8:   Assume a Mercedes car costs €90,000 and the exchange rate is £1 = €1.25. Calculate the selling price in pounds in the UK required to return €90,000 to Germany.

....

Q9: Assume the exchange rate changes. The pound strengthens and £1 will now buy €1.50. Calculate the selling price in pounds in the UK now required to return €90,000 to Germany.

....

We can conclude that Mercedes can cut their price in the UK to £60,000 or increase their profit on each car sold in the UK by a further £12,000. Possibly they will do a bit of both - cutting price by a portion and increasing profits. This shows how dramatic changes in profits and price competitiveness can be when exchange rates move.

3.5 The effect of a rising exchange rate on inflation, economic growth and employment

The effect of a rising exchange rate on inflation

The previous section established that importers are able to reduce their prices when the exchange rate rises. In the example, BMWs and Mercedes were going to be cheaper in the UK. Imports are items we buy and therefore feature in the consumer price index (CPI) which is the measure of inflation. If some items in the CPI are reduced in price then the index will rise more slowly so inflation slows down.

The effects on UK companies may include:

- seeking new ways to reduce costs or accept a profit cut to remain competitive. They may also reduce prices. Therefore, at least for internationally traded goods, a rising exchange rate will cut inflation;

- having to lay off workers if their sales reduce. This will reduce demand in the economy, and again slow down inflation;

- UK producers using components and raw materials from abroad. As the cost of these reduces, UK companies may pass these savings on to customers by reducing their prices.

The effect of a rising exchange rate on economic growth and employment

UK exporters are going to struggle to remain competitive abroad. In home markets, imports are going to have a competitive edge. These are conditions that will lead to many UK firms cutting costs to survive. They will look at all their operations and assess. The conclusions they are likely to come to will involve closing less efficient plants and looking to reduce labour costs through redundancies. Words like "restructuring", "rationalisation", "downsizing" and "delayering" will occur frequently in the business pages. The weakest UK firms and those slow to adjust will go out of business.

Other effects may include:

- jobs will be lost, economic growth will slow down and there is the possibility of recession. The danger then is that recession drags down even efficient firms as a negative multiplier effect takes hold on the general economy;

- on a more positive note, the slowdown may not go as far as recession and during the process UK productivity will rise under the competitive pressures and a leaner, more efficient UK economy will emerge;

- when the least efficient go out of business, average productivity in the economy can be expected to improve as only the most efficient survive.

The effect of a rising exchange rate on inflation, economic growth and employment

Go online

Q10: A rising exchange rate makes our exports more *(expensive/cheaper)*, and our imports *(expensive/cheaper)*. This *(increases/decreases)* unemployment because UK goods are *(less/more)* price competitive in world markets. With less output economic growth *(increases/decreases)*, and combined with a *(negative/positive)* multiplier effect, there is a danger of *(inflation/recession)*.

. . . .

3.6 The effect of a falling exchange rate on individuals, firms and the current account

A falling exchange rate logically works in the opposite way to a rising exchange rate. As a student, you have a shortcut to completing your understanding of the effects of changing exchange rates.

If you have followed the reasoning in the previous sections on rising exchange rates, it should not be difficult to work out the effects of a falling exchange rate. Let us fill in some missing words to check your understanding.

The effect of a falling exchange rate

Go online

Q11: Complete the paragraph by choosing the correct words from the following list:

- employment;
- exports;
- growth;
- imports;
- inflation;
- more;
- raise.

A falling exchange rate for the pound will make our .... cheaper and our .... more expensive. This will make UK exporters .... price competitive. In home markets foreign firms will be under pressure to .... prices. As a result UK firms may increase output thus increasing economic .... This will create more .... in the UK. However the cost of imports will make .... higher.

. . . .

To summarise the effects of a falling exchange rate:

- Inflation will tend to rise because of the rising costs of imported goods and services, and the rising price of imported raw materials and components. If rising inflation encourages expectations of future inflation then trade unions will demand higher wage rises and inflation in the UK economy could become built-in and difficult to reduce.

- UK exporters will enjoy a price advantage in foreign markets. In the home market, it will be harder for imports to remain competitive. Both of these outcomes of a falling exchange rate will increase sales by UK firms and hence UK output. Faster economic growth will lead to higher employment.

3.7 Fixed exchange rates

An **exchange rate that is fixed** will be set by a central bank at a level which it intends will be maintained. This will involve agreements with other central banks so that an appropriate level can be agreed for each exchange rate in a fixed system. Historically the best example was the gold standard. Each country's currency was exchangeable at the central bank for a fixed weight of gold. In effect this fixed the relative values of currencies. Britain abandoned the gold standard in 1931.

More recently in the run-up to the creation of the Euro currency, there was a period when the currencies lining up to convert to the euro sought to maintain their values against each other. This process of "convergence" was similar to a fixed exchange rate system as central banks sought to maintain approximate levels within the European Exchange Rate Mechanism (ERM) and to narrow down the fluctuations between these currencies. There were several realignments along the way, so "fixed" is better thought of as "flexible". When these currencies were finally traded in for euros, this was in a sense a permanent fix of these exchange rates. Fixed so firmly that they vanished and became one.

The advantages of fixed exchange rates

Fixed exchange rates could be claimed to have the following benefits:

- Speculators, for long periods, accept these exchange rates in the knowledge that concerted action from central banks will maintain them making successful speculation difficult.

- Stability is created for business in international markets, encouraging trade and foreign investment as there is certainty that unpredictable currency movements will not impact on profits.

- The soft option for governments of devaluing a currency to recover price competitiveness is not easily available. Rather, they must address underlying economic problems such as inflation or low productivity.

The disadvantages of fixed exchange rates

Speculators over time will notice the divergence of different economies. They will appreciate that the prevailing fixed exchange rates are historic. Some economies will advance rapidly with export-led economic growth and increasing productivity. The relative position of other economies will decline. A shift sooner or later will have to occur in the fixed exchange rates.

Speculators (who always understand economics) will see the opportunity of a one-way bet. As there is only one possible direction for an exchange rate in a fast advancing economy to go, they will begin buying this currency (and selling currencies of countries with the least positive economic outlook). If they are wrong it will probably just be in the timing, and meanwhile they can always extract their money from the foreign exchange market at no loss. This is a bet you can win without much risk: a one-way bet.

Stability in currency markets as a generator of international trade can easily be over-rated. Markets have developed, such as the futures market, where companies can fix the currency value for their trade. Speculators then take the risk of any ups and downs in the currency, and the company knows exactly what it will receive from its foreign transaction. Note that speculators perform a useful function in markets when they take on risk.

On the issue of devaluing a currency being a soft option - if repeated devaluations occur that is perhaps so. However, as an alternative to stringent fiscal or monetary policies, taking the so-called soft option may be an effective escape route for a troubled economy, allowing it to avoid unemployment. Why reduce the number of economic options available to a country? **Devaluation** should be considered on its merits as a possible breathing space for an economy while issues of low productivity are addressed.

Central banks require to hold large reserves of gold and foreign currency to use for intervention in the market to defend fixed exchange rates.

Go online

Fixed exchange rates

Q12: Complete the paragraph by choosing the correct words from the following list:

- automatically;
- central;
- certainty;
- intervention;
- profitability;
- quality;
- reserves;
- speculation.

Fixed exchange rates allow firms to trade with .... that exchange rate movements will not affect the .... of international contracts. For long periods, ... will not take place because .... banks will successfully maintain the currency value.

....

3.8 Floating exchange rates

An exchange rate that floats freely in the foreign exchange market moves according to supply and demand. A distinction is often made between a **"clean" float** and a **"dirty" float**.

A "clean" float is where the central bank does not intervene in the market as a buyer or seller of the currency. The pound sterling is a clean floating exchange rate.

A "dirty" float describes a floating exchange rate that is managed by central bank intervention in the market. The government has a clear view on what the value of its "floating" exchange rate should be. Through its central bank it buys and sells on the market to influence the currency value.

The advantages of floating exchange rates

Floating exchange rates are claimed to have the following benefits:

- They adjust constantly to the prevailing economic conditions and thus speculators are unable to spot a misalignment of the currency that would provide an opportunity for speculation.

- If large-scale intervention by a central bank to support a currency is no longer going to take place then large reserves of gold and foreign currency are not required.

- The economic problems such as inflation or unemployment that can be exacerbated by too high or too low a currency value can be avoided. The currency adjusts constantly and automatically to reflect prevailing economic conditions. The market mechanism of supply and demand is relied upon to set an appropriate exchange rate.

The disadvantages of floating exchange rates

Markets can over-shoot. Market sentiment is not the same as speculation. Markets are made up of traders and there will always be a psychological component to their behaviour. The prevailing conventional wisdom may temporarily lead markets in an inappropriate direction. Belief in the benevolence of markets should be tempered.

The steady decline of a currency over time remains an option for a government that refuses to deal with supply-side productivity problems within its economy. Allowing your currency to sink slowly may be an option taken to avoid hard decisions that address fundamental economic problems with tough fiscal, monetary or supply-side policies.

Exchange rate policy such as having a higher exchange rate to reduce inflation is no longer an option. By allowing a free float, you exclude the possibility of using the exchange rate to control your economy.

Speculators will not go away. The currencies of small countries will be particularly open to bouts of speculation. The act of speculation brings about the expected outcome. If a currency is heavily sold its price will fall. The speculators bring about the very outcome they were speculating on. In early 2008 there were rumours that the Icelandic currency was witnessing just such a bout of market manipulation.

Stability of exchange rates assists international trade. The futures market allows firms to be certain as to the exchange rate they will receive even in a world of floating exchange rates. However the speculators taking on risk by trading on the futures market will expect to return an overall profit from their dealings. Therefore using the futures market must create an extra cost for companies.

Go online

Floating exchange rates

Q13: Complete the paragraph by choosing the correct words from the following list:

- automatically;
- floating;
- intervention;
- over-shoot;
- profit;
- quality;
- reserves;
- speculators.

Floating exchange rates .... adjust to prevailing economic conditions.   No .... by central banks means that large .... of foreign currency are not required and .... find it difficult to spot an inappropriate exchange value to .... from when the rates reflect prevailing economic conditions.

....

3.9   Exchange rate systems summary

Go online

Exchange rate systems

For each question on exchange rate systems, decide if the scenario is an advantage for a fixed or a floating exchange rate.

Q14: Controlling inflation with a high exchange rate.

a) Advantage for fixed exchange rate
b) Advantage for floating exchange rate

....

Q15: Reducing the need for gold and currency reserves.

a) Advantage for fixed exchange rate
b) Advantage for floating exchange rate

....

Q16: Automatic adjustment to reflect state of economy.

a) Advantage for fixed exchange rate
b) Advantage for floating exchange rate

. . . .

Q17: Stability and certainty that encourages trade.

a) Advantage for fixed exchange rate
b) Advantage for floating exchange rate

. . . .

3.10   Trends in the pound to dollar exchange rate - a historical perspective

The exchange rate between the UK pound and the US dollar is one of the longest established in history. The table below shows a selection of the figures over the years from 1791.

Year	$s to £s	Notes
1791	4.55	Earliest available figure
1875	5.59	High point of nineteenth century
1900	4.87	End of Nineteenth Century
1934	4.93	During the Great Depression
1942	4.04	Middle of World War 2
1950	2.80	This rate was maintained until the late 1960s
1970	2.40	After devaluation of 1960s
1977	1.75	1970s low point

Go online

Trends in the pound to dollar exchange rate

Q18: From the table below of recent dollar to pound exchange rates produce a line graph for the years 1992 to 2014. This can be done on MS Excel or by hand.

Year	Rate	Year	Rate
1992	1.77	2004	1.83
1993	1.50	2005	1.82
1994	1.53	2006	1.84
1995	1.58	2007	2.00
1996	1.56	2008	1.85
1997	1.64	2009	1.57
1998	1.66	2010	1.55
1999	1.62	2011	1.60
2000	1.52	2012	1.58
2001	1.44	2013	1.56
2002	1.50	2014	1.56
2003	1.64	2015	n/a

. . . .

3.11 Summary

Summary

At the end of this topic students should know that:

- an exchange rate is the price of one currency in terms of another currency;
- the pound is demanded when:
    - the UK's exports are purchased;
    - tourists come to the UK;
    - foreign companies invest in the UK;
    - the Bank of England supports it by buying pounds;
    - UK interest rates increase;
- the pound is supplied when:
    - UK consumers purchase imports;
    - UK tourists go abroad;
    - UK companies invest abroad;
    - the Bank of England sells pounds;
    - UK interest rates decrease;
- the exchange rate has implications for individuals, firms and the current account of the balance of payments;
- a fixed exchange rate system offers stability and certainty about returns and encourages trade and international investment. If the fixed rate begins to look untenable then speculators will profit by taking positions in advance of an inevitable devaluation or revaluation;
- a floating exchange rate in theory adjusts automatically to the prevailing economic conditions. Market sentiment can change and the adjustment process can be quite rapid;
- the volatility of currencies as shown by the pound / dollar exchange rate over time.

3.12   End of topic test

Go online

End of Topic 3 test

The UK has decided not to join the Eurozone and will continue to allow sterling to float. One reason for this is that joining the Eurozone would result in a large fall in the UK rate of interest. *(SQA 2007)*

Q19: The demand for the pound increases when:

a) exports from the UK increase.
b) UK tourists go abroad.
c) the Bank of England lowers interest rates.
d) there is expectation that the pound will devalue.

. . . .

Q20: Other things being equal, a fall in the exchange rate of the pound should:

a) decrease employment.
b) decrease inflation.
c) increase imports.
d) increase exports.

. . . .

Q21: Compared to floating exchange rates, fixed exchange rates have the problem that:

a) as economies grow at different rates, they become unsustainable.
b) international business contracts are more difficult to conclude.
c) Both of the above.
d) Neither of the above.

. . . .

Q22: If the UK joined the eurozone, it would lose independent control of:

a) taxation.
b) transport infrastructure.
c) government spending.
d) interest rates.

. . . .

Q23: The demand for a currency with speculative 'hot money' will depend on:

a) relative interest rates being high for that currency.
b) the risk of a fall in the exchange rate of that currency being low.
c) Both of the above.
d) Neither of the above.

. . . .

Q24: Explain factors that determine the demand for sterling on the foreign exchange markets.

(8 marks)

. . . .

Q25: Discuss the advantages and disadvantages for a country of having a floating exchange rate.

(10 marks)

. . . .

Q26: Explain some of the economic problems that could result from a large fall in the UK rate of interest.

(7 marks)

. . . .

Topic 4

The balance of payments

Contents

Prerequisite knowledge

This topic assumes no previous knowledge and is intended to be accessible for those studying Economics for the first time. However, if you have already completed National 5 Economics, you will be familiar with some of the concepts outlined.

Learning objectives

By the end of this topic you should be able to:

- *be able to define the terms balance of payments, current account and capital account;*

- *be able to explain the components of the current account of the balance of payments;*

- *understand the trade terms visibles and invisibles;*

- *be able to explain the components of the capital and financial account of the balance of payments;*

- *understand the reasons why the balance of payments may move into surplus or deficit;*

- *be familiar with trends in the balance of payments over the last 10 years, and the reasons for these trends;*

- *be able to explain the methods that can be used to reduce current account deficits.*

4.1   Definition of the balance of payments

The economic transactions of UK residents with the rest of the world are recorded in an account called the **balance of payments**. It also shows how these transactions are funded.

Items in the balance of payments include:

- exports and imports of goods;
- exports and imports of services;
- dividends and interest paid across national boundaries (**income flows**);
- international investment flows in and out of the UK (**financial flows**);
- foreign aid and transfers to and from international organisations such as the European Union (**transfers**).

The balance of payments is a balance sheet. As an accountant will tell you, a balance sheet is supposed to balance. Every transaction that goes into a balance sheet is subject to a system called double entry accounting. The value of the item purchased is entered on one side of the accounts and how you paid for it (the same value) is entered on the other side. An accountant would say that "every debit has a credit". Therefore technically, the final figures on the balance of payments always balance. When it doesn't, an entry '**errors and omissions**' is made to force the balance.

The balance of payments is divided into two sections:

- the **current account**;
- the **capital and financial account**.

An example of the layout of the balance of payments with the main components highlighted is shown below.

	Credits (exports in £ million)	Debits (imports in £ million)
1. Current account		
A. Goods and services	369,691	424,128
B. Income	241,350	222,795
C. Current transfers	16,165	28,064
Total current account	**627,206**	**674,987**
2. Capital and financial accounts		
A. Capital account	3,818	2,988
B. Financial account	687,387	654,582
Total capital and financial accounts	**691,205**	**657,570**

Total (totals of current account + capital and financial account)	1,318,411	1,332,557
Net errors and omissions	14,146	
Balance	**1,332,557**	**1,332,557**

Pink Book - balance of payment figures

The latest figures for the UK's balance of payments can be researched in the UK Government's annual 'Pink Book' of balance of payments details. The Pink Book can be accessed on the internet.

Locate the balance of payments figures for the most recent available year and present them in a table as in the example above. Be prepared to read carefully through the contents list to find the correct page.

Note: There is no definitive solution to this exercise as it will depend on the year.

4.2   Definition of current account

The current account measures income flows during the year. The most significant items in this section are payments for exports and imports of both goods and services.

Non-trade items in the current account include investment income (repatriation of profits and dividends). The transfer of interest payments from money in overseas accounts is also included in the current account. You may see this summarised as IPD (interest, profits and dividends).

The term 'transfers' is used to describe:

- overseas aid;

- contributions to the budgets of international organisations (e.g. the European Union);

- money sent overseas by immigrant workers to their families.

The current account on the UK balance of payments

Watch the video from the UK Government's Office of National Statistics for further information about the current account - http://youtu.be/cbJIVmsKOZU ('The Current Account on the UK Balance of Payments - Explained') .

Go online

4.3   Component elements of the current account

Goods are tangible objects.   Goods of all sorts are termed **'visibles'** in trade talk, presumably because you possess the object and can look at it or show it to somebody else. The difference between visible exports and visible imports has a particular title. It is called the **balance of trade**.

The UK balance of trade has rarely been in the black (visible exports greater than visible imports) in recent history. Balance of trade deficits are the norm for the UK.

Services are also traded. Curiously, they are termed **'invisibles'** in trade terminology. It does seem a little strange to be counting invisibles. Services are quite difficult to describe other than by giving examples. Often they are said to be intangible, which at least has the advantage of being easily remembered if goods are tangible.

A service generates a receipt or an accounting entry. If you buy insurance for your Greek owned, Panamanian registered, oil tanker at Lloyds in London, you will pay the UK company for the insurance. They will give you an insurance document in return and ring the Lutine Bell if it sinks! As the service has been provided by a UK company and the price charged is paid into the UK, this would count as an invisible export.

The UK invisible balance has been in surplus (invisible exports exceed invisible imports) for many years.

Go online

Visible or invisible

For each item below, decide if it is a visible or invisible.

Q1:   Cars

a)   Visible
b)   Invisible

. . . .

Q2:   Tourism

a)   Visible
b)   Invisible

. . . .

Q3:   Banking

a)   Visible
b)   Invisible

. . . .

Q4:   Bananas

a)   Visible
b)   Invisible

. . . .

Visibles

Q5: Complete the final column in the following table.

Go online

Year	Export of goods (£ billion)	Import of goods (£ billion)	Visible balance (£ billion)
2010	271	368	
2011	309	406	
2012	305	414	
2013	307	419	
2014	292	412	

....

Q6: Present the figures from your table in a line graph. You may do this by hand in which case some squared paper would be a help. Alternatively if you are familiar with MS Excel and have access to it, you can prepare a chart using Excel.

....

Invisibles

Q7: Complete the final column in the following table.

Go online

Year	Export of services (£ billion)	Import of services (£ billion)	Invisible balance (£ billion)
2010	176	116	
2011	190	118	
2012	196	121	
2013	209	130	
2014	208	123	

....

Q8: Present the figures from your table in a line graph.

....

We can assemble the UK current account for 2013 as follows. (Note recent trade figures are subject to revisions and different sources can provide slightly different figures depending on when they obtained the details. This explains the slight variation between the revised figures below and earlier details for 2013.)

	Exports (in £ billion)	Imports (in £ billion)	Balance (in £ billion)
Goods	307	419	**-112**
Services	209	130	**79**
Net income and current transfers			**-39**
Current account balance			**-72**

Pink Book - trade figures

Locate the Pink Book on UK trade figures on the internet. Find the latest figures that would update the UK current account table to the latest year available.

Note: The solution will change with every year that passes, so a definitive one cannot be given.

. . . .

4.4   Surpluses and deficits

Focussing firstly on the current account section, the following can be noted. The UK has a **trade in goods deficit** - imports of goods exceed exports. The UK has a **trade in services surplus**. Combined in the current account, the total for trade in goods and services shows an overall current account deficit (imports exceed exports). This indicates that the surplus in services is smaller than the deficit in goods, thus giving an overall deficit in goods and services.

The UK imports more goods than it exports. Why does this happen? Is it important?

There are several possible reasons for this deficit:

- As a fairly densely populated island we are a net importer of food;
- Many of our natural resources (e.g. coal) have been exploited over the centuries to the extent that what is left is difficult and expensive to get at. Therefore we are a net importer of many commodities and raw materials. However, the windfall of North Sea oil does mean that trade in oil is closer to balance;
- Comparative advantage in many manufacturing industries has moved abroad where the factor inputs (e.g. labour) are cheaper. For example wages are lower in the Far East;
- Some calculations suggest the UK economy has lower productivity (efficiency) than, for example, the USA or Germany. These international comparisons are fraught with calculation problems so this cannot be relied upon;
- The value of the pound has at certain times been unhelpfully high. This makes

import prices cheaper and our export prices dearer. In early 2008 the pound was high against the dollar making exporting to the USA difficult. In 2014, the pound has again risen, reflecting a recovery in the UK economy;

- There have been question marks in the past over the quality of management and the quality of design in this country, although improvement has occurred in both these areas;

- Investment in modern capital can be lower than in many other countries.

Much of the deficit in goods is made up by a surplus in services, thus reducing the size of the overall current account deficit. The UK has a comparative advantage in financial services based on the activities of the City of London. Edinburgh is also a significant financial centre. The UK attracts inflows of capital investment.

There is no special significance attached to trade in goods. Services have the same potential to generate income and employment - perhaps more.

The UK's comparative advantage in some services is related to the high level of education required, and possibly to English being the international business language. A long history of activity in financial services ensures we have the suitably qualified personnel, and the infrastructure that gives some external economies of scale for bases in London. Weak regulation of financial services and a favourable tax regime may also be factors.

When the television news speaks of a trade deficit of several billion pounds, non-economists may worry that the government has to pay this money (from taxes) to foreign countries and that in some sense we are losing out. This is incorrect. As an economics student, you will realise that the trade deficit is a private sector matter. When you bought that Sony or Volkswagen product you handed over the money to pay for it. The UK government does not have to pay again. The trade deficit does not mean that the government pays again for goods you have already bought.

Surpluses and deficits

Q9: Complete the paragraph by choosing the correct words from the following list:

Go online

- capital;
- current;
- deficit;
- financial services;
- high;
- London;
- surplus;
- wages.

The UK has a .... in trade in goods, but a smaller .... in trade in services. Taken together the overall UK .... account is in deficit. Two factors causing this are low .... overseas and a £ exchange rate that for periods can be .... Fortunately the UK enjoys net .... inflows and has a strong .... sector based around the pre-eminence of ....

....

4.5   Methods of reducing current account deficits

The holy grail of economic policy in this area is export-led growth of the type enjoyed by Germany. This requires a highly efficient economy, the output of which competes successfully in world markets. Supply side policies are aimed at improving the competitiveness of the UK economy.

The following can address a current account deficit:

- Fiscal policies that act to slow the economy such as increasing taxation or cutting back on government spending act to improve the balance of payments for the same reason a recession did - less aggregate demand means less demand for imports;

- Monetary policies that curtail demand such as higher interest rates work in a similar way;

- Devaluation of the pound. If the exchange rate of the pound falls then UK exporters can cut prices in foreign currency and still receive the same return in pounds. Exports are encouraged and the converse effect reduces imports;

- Increased productivity in UK firms enables our goods and services to compete better in markets at home and abroad;

- Supply-side measures can make our economy more flexible and adaptable may give us a competitive edge.

In recession, UK consumers buy less of everything, including fewer imports. Thus while many economic variables point in an adverse direction in recession at least the balance of payments should improve.

Pink Book - current account trends

Locate the Pink Book on UK trade figures on the internet. Analyse the current account trends over the last ten years.

Note: The solution will vary as years pass. The underlying trend for some years has been a trade in goods deficit that is greater than the trade in services surplus. The trend in individual sections such as oil can be interesting. Note that the UK is no longer self-sufficient in oil. You should look for other interesting trends and contemplate why they have come about.

....

4.6   Capital and financial account

The capital and financial account (previously known as the capital account) measures money flows that are connected to investment and savings.

The capital and financial account includes foreign direct investment. This happens when a company builds an overseas factory. It is capital investment in fixed assets, that will generate current account money flows for years ahead. An example of this is the Japanese based firm Nissan building a factory in Sunderland. It works in both directions as UK based firms also invest overseas.

'Portfolio investment' is the purchase of shares in foreign firms, and is also in the capital and financial account.

'Other investment' is the label attached to financial hot money flows and this section can be volatile.

Changes in the UK's official reserves of gold and foreign currency are also recorded in this section.

Costs and benefits of foreign direct investment

Q10: Describe the costs and benefits of foreign direct investment for the Scottish economy. *(SQA 2004)*

Go online

(10 Marks)

....

4.7   Trends in the current account

The following is an extract from the annual reference for trade figures, 'The Pink Book 2014'. It covers trade figures up to 2013:

"The UK has recorded a current account deficit in every year since 1984. From 1984, the current account deficit increased steadily to reach a high of £24.7 billion in 1989. This is equivalent to 4.7% of Gross Domestic Product (GDP). From 1990 until 1997, the current account deficit narrowed to a low of £1.3 billion in 1997, equivalent to 0.1% of GDP.
Between 1998 and 2008, it widened sharply, peaking at £56.4 billion in 2008. The current account deficit narrowed over the following three years to reach £27.0 billion in 2011, before widening significantly in 2012 when it recorded a deficit of £61.9 billion.
In 2013, the deficit reached a record £72.4 billion, the highest recorded in cash terms. It was equivalent to 4.2% of GDP, the highest since 1989 (4.7%)."

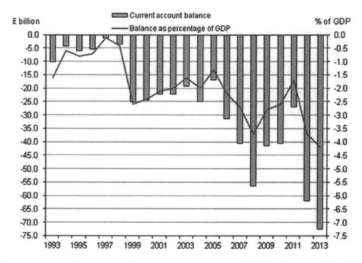

'Current account balance and balance as percentage of GDP' taken from 'The Pink Book 2014' (http://bit.ly/194PvEA). Licensed under Open Government Licence v3.0 (http://bit.ly/1uzupHL) via The National Archives.

Trends in the current account

Q11: Summarise the trends illustrated in the graph (above).

Go online

....

Q12: Research online the latest year available and print out a note of the up-to-date version of the statistics and summary shown in the graph (above).

....

4.8   Trends in the trade in goods and services

The trade in goods account recorded net surpluses in 1980 to 1982, largely due to the growth in exports of North Sea oil. Since then, the trade in goods account has remained in deficit. The deficit grew significantly in the late 1980s to reach a peak of £25.2 billion in 1989, before narrowing in the early 1990s to levels of around £10 billion to £14 billion.

In 1998, the deficit jumped by £9.5 billion to £22.2 billion and increased in every year since, except for 2009 and 2011. In 2013, the deficit reached £110.2 billion.

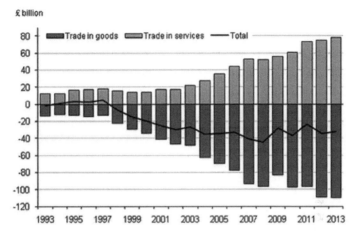

'Trade in goods and services balances' taken from 'The Pink Book 2014' (http://bit.ly/194PvEA). Licensed under Open Government Licence v3.0 (http://bit.ly/1uzupHL) via The National Archives.

Trends in the trade in goods and services

Q13: Summarise the trends illustrated in the graph (above).

....

Go online

4.9   Summary

Summary

At the end of this topic students should know that:

- the definition of the relevant terms:
  - balance of payments;
  - current account;
  - capital and financial account;
- the components of the balance of payments;
- visible trade (goods) and invisible trade (services) are the main parts of the current account;
- income flows from previous investments abroad are also in the current account;
- the UK has a deficit in visible trade, and a surplus in invisible trade;
- the reasons why a deficit may occur;
- fiscal, monetary and supply-side policies can all be used to reduce a balance of payments deficit;
- the latest trends in the UK balance of payments.

4.10   End of topic test

End of Topic 4 test

Go online

Q14: The current account of the balance of payments includes:

a) portfolio investment.
b) hot money flows.
c) trade in services.
d) flows to and from reserves of foreign currency.

....

Q15: The UK's trade in goods and trade in services:

a) are both in deficit.
b) are both in surplus.
c) show a deficit for goods and a surplus for services.
d) show a surplus for goods and a deficit for services.

....

Q16: Current account deficits could be improved by:

a) improving productivity.
b) devaluing the pound.
c) Both of the above.
d) Neither of the above.

....

Q17: The capital and financial account of the balance of payments includes:

a) trade in goods.
b) trade in services.
c) foreign direct investment.
d) interest, profits and dividends.

....

Q18: The categories 'trade in goods' and 'trade in services' are also generally referred to as (respectively):

a) visibles and invisibles.
b) tangibles and intangibles.
c) physicals and non-physicals.
d) exports and imports.

....

In 2004, the UK had a trade in goods deficit of £61 billion and a budget deficit of £37 billion. *(SQA 2006)*

Q19: Explain the difference between a trade in goods deficit and a budget deficit.

(4 marks)

....

Q20: Explain how budget deficits can lead to increased trade deficits and decreased unemployment.

(8 marks)

. . . .

Q21: Other than budget deficits, suggest and explain two reasons for the UK's large trade in goods deficits in recent years.

(6 marks)

. . . .

. . . .

Topic 5

Understanding the impact of the global economy

Contents

Prerequisite knowledge

This topic assumes no previous knowledge and is intended to be accessible for those studying Economics for the first time. However, if you have already completed National 5 Economics you will be familiar with some of the concepts outlined.

Learning objectives

By the end of this topic you should be able to:

- *discuss the pros and cons of the UK joining the euro;*

- *explain the role of the European Central Bank;*

- *describe the process of enlargement and explain the advantages and disadvantages enlargement may bring the UK;*

- *explain the role of the common external tariff;*
- *describe the economic characteristics of an emerging economy;*
- *explain the policies that may lead to economic development;*
- *describe the economic characteristics of a developing country;*
- *discuss the merits of aid and trade to developing countries.*

5.1 The European Union (EU) - introduction

The European Union was founded in 1957. Before that in 1951 the six original members formed the European Steel and Coal Community, out of which grew the European Union. For the next few decades it was generally called the 'common market' in the non-member United Kingdom. The UK joined in 1973.

The European Union is a free trade area of 28 countries and over 500 million consumers. For a long period it was called the European Economic Community (EEC), but in recognition of it developing beyond just an economic union, the middle word was dropped and it became plain EU.

We will consider four aspects of the EU. These are:

- **the eurozone**;
- **enlargement**;
- **the European Central Bank**;
- **the common external tariff**.

5.2 The eurozone

By 2015 the number of members of the euro had grown to 19. Twelve of the EU members started using the euro on 1 January 2002. These countries formed the eurozone and pooled their monetary policy.

A single currency requires only a single interest rate. The European Central Bank was created to manage a eurozone-wide monetary policy.

The eurozone

Q1: From the following list of 28 EU countries put the 19 countries in the eurozone into the table below: Austria; Belgium; Bulgaria; Croatia; Cyprus; Czech Republic; Denmark; Estonia; Finland; France; Germany; Greece; Hungary; Ireland; Italy; Latvia; Lithuania; Luxembourg; Malta; Netherlands; Poland; Portugal; Romania; Slovakia; Slovenia; Spain; Sweden; United Kingdom.

Go online

Eurozone countries

....

5.2.1 The advantages and disadvantages of joining the euro for the UK

The advantages of joining the euro for the UK are similar to the benefits of the single currency which are that:

- it reduces the risk for UK firms that adverse exchange rate fluctuations will affect profits;

- it removes conversion costs for firms and tourists (no need to exchange currency and pay commission);

- it is expected that a European Central Bank will be firm on inflation;

- it will create **price transparency** so that consumers can easily compare prices across the EU;

- it is more likely that the UK would continue to attract foreign investment because the uncertainty of fluctuating exchange rates when exporting to the EU is removed;

- the UK's flexible labour markets should help it be successful within the eurozone.

The disadvantages of joining the euro include:

- the initial costs of changing currency are large - slot machine changes are one example.

- a need for the UK economy to become largely **convergent** with the existing eurozone. Key economic indicators such as stage of the business cycle and inflation will need to be broadly in line with the existing eurozone members. Otherwise you will be joining a currency with an inappropriate interest rate - hardly a good start!

- losing control of monetary policy. The UK will have little influence with the European Central Bank and the interest rate it sets could be out of line with UK economic needs. (It could be argued that the current UK interest rate is typically set in response to the needs of the south-east of Britain and rarely reflects the economic needs of other parts of the UK - so little difference for the Western Isles, then.)

- devaluation is removed from the UK's economic policy options, so the UK will no longer be able to stimulate its economy by devaluing its currency and increasing exports.

- the significance of interest rate changes for the UK economy is greater because of the UK's focus on house purchase, rather than rental. The UK is more sensitive to interest rate changes than other countries. This adds weight to the argument to retain control of interest rates by not joining the eurozone.

- increased regional aid within Europe will be needed to offset economic inequalities that can no longer be addressed through national currency realignments. As one of the richer nations the UK may be a net contributor of this funding.

- if some eurozone members increase their borrowings and national debt, this will lead to the single interest rate rising throughout the zone.

- the euro is essentially a fixed exchange rate arrangement, and in time may be subject to the same pressures from diverging economies that fixed rates have always been subject to. In early 2008 it was reported that, with Spain moving towards recession, there were already those arguing to leave the euro.

Joining the euro - advantages and disadvantages for the UK

Go online

Q2: Place the following advantages and disadvantages for the UK of joining the euro into the appropriate column:

- Easier for consumers to compare prices in different countries;
- No commission on changing currency;
- One interest rate set for all of eurozone;
- Exchange rate certainty for firms within eurozone;
- Devaluation of the pound no longer possible;
- Multinational investment in UK more likely.

Advantages of joining the euro	Disadvantages of joining the euro

....

5.3 European Central Bank (ECB)

The European Central Bank is the monetary authority for the eurozone. It performs a role in setting interest rates that is similar to the Bank of England's role as the UK's central bank.

As the central bank for the euro currency, the ECB's central aim is to maintain the purchasing power of the euro by setting an interest rate that ensures low inflation across the eurozone.

European Central Bank building in Frankfurt (http://bit.ly/1D4BjGl) by ArcCan (http://bit.ly/1AzmTie). Licensed under CC BY-SA 3.0 (http://bit.ly/18TLJ0u) via Wikimedia Commons.

5.4   EU enlargement

EU enlargement is the process of widening the EU through the admission of new members. Initially progress was slow with only nine members until 1981. The former dictatorships of Greece, Spain and Portugal then joined as democracies in the 1980s. Austria, Finland and Sweden made it fifteen. In the case of Austria and Finland, the break-up of their powerful communist neighbour the Soviet Union made it politically easier to join what had until then been a Western European club.

The waning control and influence of the Soviet Union and emergence from communism led to a wave of east European countries joining in 2004. The islands of Malta and Cyprus also joined at this time. In 2007 Rumania and Bulgaria made 27 nations of what had been 15 just over 3 years earlier. Croatia is the first member from the breakup of Yugoslavia to join (2013) and that makes 28 members.

The table summarises when countries joined the EU in ascending order of years. Note that the unification of East and West Germany in 1990 did not add an extra member.

Year	Nations joining	Total membership
1957	Belgium, France, Italy, Luxembourg, Netherlands, West Germany	6
1973	Denmark, Eire, United Kingdom	9
1981	Greece	10
1986	Portugal, Spain	12
1990	Unification of East and West Germany	12
1995	Austria, Finland, Sweden	15
2004	Cyprus, Czech Republic, Estonia, Hungary, Latvia, Lithuania, Malta, Poland, Slovakia, Slovenia	25
2007	Bulgaria, Rumania	27
2013	Croatia	28

Around the edges of the current map, below, the Balkan states formed on the break-up of Yugoslavia will shortly be looking for entry (e.g. Croatia may be followed by others such as Serbia). Turkey has long been interested, but is perhaps not as close to membership now as a few years ago. North African countries just across the Mediterranean have historic links to many European countries and are also possible members.

Switzerland retains an independent outlook and has historically sought to remain neutral. Norway voted against entry when its Scandinavian neighbours joined. It has a small population similar to Scotland and its immense oil reserves make it very prosperous outside the EU. Also, its important fishing industry does not have to abide by EU policies.

EU member states using the euro (Eurozone)
ERM II member states
States which have unilaterally adopted the euro
Other EU member states

Eurozone and EU member states

5.4.1 The benefits and problems of enlargement for the UK

For the UK the process of enlargement has several benefits:

- consumers will have a greater choice of products, as new members begin to export to the UK;

- it increases competition. Competition drives down prices, leads to innovative behaviour by firms, and can improve the quality of products;

- it allows labour shortages to be met with foreign workers. This addition to supply in the labour market will help to keep down wage inflation. Good news for companies and a benefit for the overall economy;

- it provides new markets (no trade barriers) for our exports, and exporters should gain more from economies of scale as they supply a free trade **single market** of over 500 million consumers;

- it provides opportunities for UK based firms to improve profitability by moving to the lower wage economies of the new members.

Enlargement can create problems for the UK:

- UK workers will face more competition in the labour market and their wages are less likely to rise (however, unemployment may not rise, because much of the money earned by foreign workers will be spent in the UK and thus they create jobs as well as take jobs);
- subsidies for the economic development of the new members may be expensive for richer countries such as the UK. The UK will be a net contributor to the EU budget through the **CAP** and regional aid;
- firms may move manufacturing to the new member countries to take advantage of lower costs (e.g. wages) and this will lead to some job losses in the UK.

Go online

Enlargement of the EU - benefits and problems for the UK

Q3:   Place the following benefits and problems for the enlargement of the EU into the appropriate column:

- Additional EU budget costs for the UK;
- Wider markets for UK goods;
- Increased choice for UK consumers;
- Multinationals move to cheaper locations;
- Skilled workers from abroad to fill vacancies.

Benefits of enlargement for the UK	Problems of enlargement for the UK

5.5   Common Customs Tariff (CCT)

A tariff is a tax on imports. It makes imports less price competitive in the EU market. The Common Customs Tariff (CCT) is often referred to as the common external tariff. It applies to the import of goods across the external border of the EU. The tariff rates do vary according to the kind of import.

The EU claims that the tariff ensures that EU domestic producers are able to compete fairly against imports from non-EU countries.   Others may regard it as a form of protectionism.   It does have serious implications for the economies of developing countries by making it harder to sell in the affluent EU market.

5.6   Levels of development

There are many labels given to groups of economies at different stages of development. Some of these labels even overlap each other. A selection of labels would include: "tiger economies", "big emerging market economies" (BEMs), first world nations, industrialised nations, less economically developed countries (LEDCs) and most economically developed countries (MEDCs).

To clarify the position, only three will be used in this section, namely:

- **developing countries**;
- **emerging economies**;
- **developed countries**.

The United Nations has an index for measuring the level of development of a nation. It combines life expectancy at birth, knowledge and education, and the standard of living. Combining these three components gives the **Human Development Index (HDI)**.

Knowledge and education is mainly judged through adult literacy rates which have a two thirds weighting in that section, with the level of enrolment in the education system as the other factor.

Standard of living is measured as gross domestic product *per capita*.

The HDI top five nations in 2007 were listed as: Norway, Iceland, Australia, Luxembourg and Canada. The United Kingdom came fifteenth.

Of the countries that contributed information to allow the calculation of the index, the bottom five nations were: Chad, Mali, Burkino Faso, Sierra Leone and Niger, occupying places 174th to 178th respectively.

Human Development Index (HDI) of the countries of the world

A variety of websites contain maps showing the Human Development Index (HDI) of the countries of the world.

Go online

Use a search engine, such as Google, entering the keywords "hdi map". Note where the majority of developing countries and where the majority of less developed countries are located. Check your findings with your teacher and tutor.

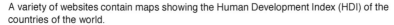

Levels of development

Q4:   Consider the statistics in the table below.

Decide whether each country is developing, emerging or developed.

Go online

Nation	Income per person ($)	Life Expectancy (years)	Literacy Rate (%)	Developing/ Emerging/ Developed
Malawi	900	60	75	
India	4,000	68	63	
Bangladesh	2,100	71	58	
Japan	37,100	84	99	
South Africa	11,500	50	93	
Sweden	40,900	82	99	
Chad	2,500	49	35	
United Kingdom	37,300	80	99	
Brazil	12,100	73	90	

. . . .

World Factbook

Go the CIA website (http://www.cia.gov) and click the "World Factbook" link. Click on some regions on the interactive map to find statistics for countries from different parts of the world, choosing different countries from those used in the previous activity (above).

In the statistics for your chosen countries, go to the 'Economy' and the 'People and society' sections and search for GDP per capita (i.e. income per person), life expectancy, and literacy rate.

Make these items into a table as in the example from the previous activity (above).

. . . .

5.7   Developing countries

Developing countries can be identified by items such as average income, life expectancy and literacy rate. These are outcomes created by the weaknesses developing countries have with their resource inputs. Looking at the factors of production (resources) one by one, it will be possible to spot problems with either the quantity of each factor or the quality of it.

It is a good idea, for memorising, to organise your thoughts in a systematic way. When it comes to the problems facing less developed countries, one approach is to take the four factors of production in turn and recite quality and quantity issues they face:

1. **Natural resources** (land) will not be fertile. Either the climate or the soil type will prevent it from producing plenty. If it is fertile, then it may be prone to seasonal flooding or drought. Crop yields will either be low, or not reliable.

Mineral deposits will be limited, or difficult to access. Those mines that do exist will be owned by multi-nationals and the workers may be poorly paid with the profits going to shareholders in developed countries.

2. **Human resources** (labour) will not be skilled. The education system will be poor and literacy rates low. As a result labour productivity will be low, and foreign investment will not be attracted. Workers may be weakened by malnutrition or disease.

Life expectancy will be low. There may be a burgeoning young population of dependents but quite a small population of working age. The number of able workers of working age will be restricted by health issues.

3. **Man-made resources** (capital) will be of poor quality.   Operating at near subsistence level there will be no surplus put aside to assist with future production. Machinery will tend to be cheap and basic when it does exist.   The lack of social capital and infrastructure such as roads and harbours will make the country unattractive to foreign investors.

A lack of savings will lead to a lack of funds being recycled into investment. The banking system will be poor.

4. **Entrepreneurs** (enterprise) will exist on a small scale in local markets. Any excess farm output will find its way to a market stall. The growth of enterprise is dependent on the availability of capital to invest, and partly on the education levels of the entrepreneurs.

The number of entrepreneurs and the size of companies will be restricted by the small incomes of consumers.

Developing countries

Go online

Q5: Match up the following issues for developing countries with the correct factor of production. All of these items will also potentially pose problems for entrepreneurs attempting to run a business:

- Droughts leading to crop failure;
- Few natural resources;
- Lack of modern technology;
- Little is saved;
- Low literacy rates;
- Poor health;
- Poor transport infrastructure;
- Seasonal flooding;
- Unskilled workers;
- Weak banking system.

Land	Labour	Capital

. . . .

5.7.1   Longer term problems of developing countries

The problems with the four factors of production lead to longer term problems:

- **Debt** - Small incomes and little business activity mean that the tax base for the governments of less developed countries to raise income from is tiny. Governments will have budget deficits because they try to meet many demands for funds but have little income. They borrow from abroad and get into debt problems. The interest payments on their debts are an additional charge every year.

- **Political instability** - Economic weaknesses and instability lead to political problems. Corruption and bribery is endemic. Democratic governments struggle to survive and dictators with military support often take over. The little government spending that is available is siphoned of into purchasing armaments. Against this volatile backdrop, foreign investors will think long and hard before making commitments.

- **Dependence on primary products** - The economies of developing countries may have 90% of their workforce in agriculture. The main export is typically an agricultural crop, and the country's balance of trade depends on a successful harvest and world prices for that product. Sometimes a mineral is mined, but much of the profit goes overseas.

5.7.2   Developing countries - case studies

Here are statistics showing the economies of Malawi and Chad, two developing countries.

Developing country case study 1: Malawi

Age structure	0-14 years: 47%, 15-64 years: 50%, 65+ years: 3%, median age: 16.3 years
Exports	tobacco, tea, sugar, cotton, coffee, peanuts
Foreign debt	$1,556 million
GDP per capita	$900
Imports	food, petroleum products, semi-manufactures, consumer goods
Infant mortality rate	48 per thousand
Labour force by occupation	agriculture: 90%, industry and services: 10%
Life expectancy	60
Literacy rate	75%
Major infectious diseases	bacterial and protozoal diarrhoea, hepatitis A, typhoid fever, malaria, schistosomiasis
Below poverty line	53% of population

Developing country case study 2: Chad

Age structure	0-14 years: 45%, 15-64 years: 52%, 65+ years: 3%, median age: 17.2 years
Exports	oil, cattle, cotton, gum arabic
Foreign debt	$1,828 million
GDP per capita	$2,500
Imports	machinery and transport equipment, industrial goods, foodstuffs, textiles
Infant mortality rate	90 per thousand
Labour force by occupation	agriculture: 80%, industry and services: 20%
Life expectancy	49
Literacy rate	35%
Major infectious diseases	bacterial and protozoal diarrhoea, hepatitis A and E, typhoid fever, malaria, schistosomiasis
Below poverty line	80% of population

The two case studies above give a vivid account of the problems faced by developing countries. Note that, unusually for a developing country, Chad has some oil that it exports. Despite this it remains very underdeveloped.

World Factbook - Malawi and Chad

Go the World Factbook at http://www.cia.gov and check the up-to-date details for these countries for any significant progress.

....

Senegal

Go the World Factbook at http://www.cia.gov and check the up-to-date details for Senegal and answer the following questions .

Go online

Q6: What is the life expectancy in Senegal?

a) 41
b) 61
c) 81

....

Q7: What is the literacy rate in Senegal?

a) 50%
b) 60%
c) 70%

....

Q8: What is the GDP per capita in Senegal?

a) $1,100
b) $2,100
c) $3,100

....

Q9: What percentage of the population of Senegal lives below the poverty line?

a) 14%
b) 34%
c) 54%

....

Q10: What percentage of the labour force in Senegal work in agriculture?

a) 38%
b) 58%
c) 78%

....

Q11: What percentage of the population is aged under 15?

a) 33%
b) 43%
c) 53%

....

5.8 Aid versus trade

Developing countries are on a subsistence treadmill. Struggling to adequately feed and shelter their people, there is no surplus left to contribute to investment in the future. In 2007 the economy of Chad was estimated to have shrunk by 1.3% - things got worse.

There are some terms related to aid that you should be familiar with:

- **bilateral aid** given by one country to another country;

- **multilateral aid** given by an international agency such as the World Bank.

Some examples of the types of aid that may be given by developed countries are:

- emergency aid consisting of gifts of food and medicine;

- grants that, although free, may carry conditions;

- loans at commercial rates of interest;

- **'soft' loans** at low rates of interest;

- writing off past debts;

- technical assistance - such as economists seconded to their governments;

- education - financing students to attend universities in developed countries.

There are several problems associated with the methods of aid described above:

- all loans increase the debt interest, which then weighs on future government budgets;

- aid may encourage dependency rather than self-sufficiency;

- it may create problems for local businesses if they are to compete with free or subsidised products. The incentive of profit is needed by entrepreneurs;

- political corruption may stop aid reaching those in greatest need;

- bilateral aid may be **tied** to purchasing from the donor country. This may not be the best option as, for example, you might finish up with second-rate tractors;

- multilateral aid from the IMF or the World Bank usually attaches strings. Balanced budgets and free market solutions are sometimes conditions required by these organisations and in the short-run this can make the poor poorer;

- grants may be available for prestigious infrastructure projects, but will there then be any money available in future years to run and maintain the finished dams and airports.

Go online

Aid versus trade

Q12: Complete the following table by putting the correct description and problem next to the type of aid:

- Disaster relief (food and medicine);
- Economic "strings" attached (e.g. balanced budget);
- From international organisation;
- From one country to another;
- Increases debts;
- Low interest finance to assist development;
- May encourage dependency;
- Tied to buying from donor country.

Type of aid	Description	Problem
Bilateral aid		
Multilateral aid		
Emergency aid		
Soft loans		

5.8.1 The advantages of trade

Encouraging trade may be a better solution. Major economic trading areas such as the European Union have external tariffs that unfairly keep out imports from less developed countries. These less developed countries would gain from profits made by selling in developed markets. These could be re-invested and economic progress would take hold. Enterprise would be encouraged.

Jobs would be created and the tax base expanded. Foreign investment would be more likely, bringing with it technology. A positive multiplier effect would spread to other areas of the economy. The trade balance would be improved.

5.9 Emerging economies

Emerging economies are a group of nations that have rapidly growing economies but are still some way behind developed countries. In many ways the experiences of emerging economies are similar to those of the UK during its industrial revolution.

Population movements to the factories and industries of a growing urban sprawl mimic a process carried out in centuries gone by in the UK. The citizens on the move from inefficient family farms become far more productive in their new secondary or tertiary occupations. Often they will find decent accommodation in the cities beyond their means in the early years, and rather like the mill workers of nineteenth century Britain, they will live in densely peopled, sub-standard housing.

These emerging economies have reached "takeoff". No longer do they go round in circles on the subsistence treadmill. A critical mass has been reached, generating saving, consumer spending and investment. Opportunities for quick-witted entrepreneurs abound. The labour is still cheap by international standards and foreign investment builds factories and pays wages, bringing with it newer technologies and big advances in productivity.

Governments now have something to tax - company profits, consumer spending and rising incomes. Judiciously used on infrastructure - roads, railways, harbours, dams, healthcare, education - these taxes when spent are a catalyst in the mix. Governments in emerging economies still tend to borrow heavily, but instead of patching up poverty and fending off crises, now it is used to fund education, transport and health care for an upwardly mobile population.

Policies leading to economic development

What enables a country to reach this virtuous circle of economic growth and rising living standards? The first steps probably depend on political stability, raising basic literacy rates and the encouragement of small business activity. The world price of a mineral or crop that they export needs to be high enough to make profits for local farmers, or to encourage inward investment. Against this background government has to plan improvements in infrastructure that will nurture the infant industrialisation - even if it has to borrow to do so.

Much can still go wrong. The world prices for major exports may fall. Natural disasters such as flood and drought may hold back progress. Even success will bring the risk of inflation for a booming economy. Workers may demand higher wages that reduce your competitive advantage.

Emerging economies

Q13: In the following sentences, when given a choice, select the correct option.

Emerging economies such as (*Brazil/Belgium*) no longer depend on Go online
(*primary/secondary*) production. They tend to have (*low/high*) levels of spending on infrastructure. Literacy rates are (*over/under*) 50% as a result of these spending levels on education. (*Low/High*) levels of foreign investment occur, encouraged by political (*stability/instability*). GDP per capita, for example, could be (*$1,000/$10,000*) per annum and standards of living are (*rising/falling*). With (*increasing/decreasing*) levels of birth control, the age structure of emerging economies shows more people in the (*dependent/working*) age categories.

....

5.9.1   Characteristics of emerging economies

Emerging economies do not all have an identical profile, but several of the following characteristics will be found in each one:

- political stability - it may involve a strong and charismatic leader who may or may not be democratically elected. Singapore is an excellent example with its first prime minister from independence in 1959 until 1990, Lee Kwan Yew;

- free trade and open markets - encouraging trade, entrepreneurs and foreign investment;

- high levels of foreign investment and the presence of multinationals;

- a move away from dependence on primary production such as crops or mineral resources and into areas where value is added to products - manufacturing and services;

- high levels of government debt, but it is invested effectively in developing infrastructure to support and develop the economy - education, healthcare, water and sanitation;

- high rates of economic growth. Rapidly improving technology and increasing productivity of labour drive up output;

- rising standards of living;

- birth control is often encouraged in emerging economies. In the late 1960s Singapore began a "stop at two" family planning campaign encouraging sterilisation after two children and reducing economic benefits for third and fourth children.

5.9.2   Emerging economies - case studies

Here is a selection of statistics that illustrate the economies of India and Brazil, two emerging economies.

Emerging economies case study 1: India

Age structure	0-14 years: 29%, 15-64 years: 65%, 65+ years: 6%, median age: 27 years
Exports	petroleum products, precious stones, machinery
Foreign debt	$412 billion
GDP per capita	$4,000
Imports	crude oil, gems, machinery, fertiliser, iron and steel
Infant mortality rate	43 per thousand
Labour force by occupation	agriculture: 49%, industry: 20%, services: 31%
Life expectancy	43
Literacy rate	61%
Major infectious diseases	bacterial diarrhoea, hepatitis A and E, typhoid fever, malaria, dengue fever, leptospirosis, rabies
Below poverty line	30% of population

Emerging economies case study 2: Brazil

Age structure	0-14 years: 24%, 15-64 years: 68%, 65+ years: 8%, median age: 31 years
Exports	transport equipment, iron ore, soybeans, footwear, coffee, vehicles
Foreign debt	$476 billion
GDP per capita	$12,100
Imports	machinery, electrical and transport equipment, chemical products, oil, vehicle parts, electronics
Infant mortality rate	19 per thousand
Labour force by occupation	agriculture: 16%, industry: 13%, services: 71%
Life expectancy	73
Literacy rate	89%
Major infectious diseases	none
Below poverty line	21% of population

Malaysia

This is a quick quiz on the country, Malaysia. This emerging economy has some fairly typical figures for key indicators of development. See if you can pick the appropriate answers for a typical newly industrialised country.

Go online

Hint - go back and review the two case studies.

Q14: What is the life expectancy in Malaysia?

a) 65
b) 75
c) 85

. . . .

Q15: What is the literacy rate in Malaysia?

a) 53%
b) 73%
c) 93%

. . . .

Q16: What is the GDP per capita in Malaysia?

a) $7,500
b) $17,500
c) $27,500

. . . .

Q17: What percentage of the population of Malaysia lives below the poverty line?

a) 4%
b) 14%
c) 24%

. . . .

Q18: What percentage of the labour force in Malaysia work in agriculture?

a) 11%
b) 31%
c) 51%

. . . .

Q19: What percentage of the population is aged under 15?

a) 9%
b) 19%
c) 29%

. . . .

5.10 Summary

Summary

At the end of this topic students should know that:

- the euro requires eurozone members to set a single interest rate thus relinquishing national control of monetary policy. Advantages include savings in currency conversion costs and increasing price transparency;

- the European Central Bank is the monetary authority for the eurozone and sets the euro interest rate;

- enlargement to 28 countries (at the time of writing) has led to significant movements of workers from new members (e.g. Poland) to the UK. By creating a larger single market, opportunities for labour and enterprise are extended. Firms face greater competition and come under increased pressure to cut costs and lower prices which benefits consumers;

- the EU places a common external tariff on goods imported from non-EU countries;

- developing countries are the nations with the lowest incomes and are characterised by low literacy rates and low life expectancy. They are often dependent on primary production for much of their income;

- emerging economies are rapidly growing economies, diversifying into secondary and tertiary sectors. They attract investment from foreign multinationals;

- developed economies are the most advanced. Most workers are employed in the tertiary sector and standards of living are high;

- aid can provide short-term relief in emergencies. Grants and loans can be used to develop the infrastructure needed to make economic progress. Long-term progress can be encouraged by the opening up of markets such as the European Union to trade from developing countries.

5.11   End of topic test

Go online

End of topic test

Q20: If the UK joined the Eurozone, one disadvantage would be losing control of:

a) fiscal policy.
b) monetary policy.
c) Both of the above.
d) Neither of the above.

. . . .

Q21: Which one of the following groups consists of a developing country, an emerging economy, and a developed country, in that order?

a) India, Brazil, France.
b) Malawi, India, Japan.
c) Chad, Belgium, Germany.
d) Brazil, India, Sweden.

. . . .

Q22: Which of the following is **not** true of a typical emerging economy?

a) Growing significance of the secondary sector of their economy.
b) High levels of foreign investment.
c) Free trade with EU members.
d) Significant levels of debt to foreign countries.

. . . .

Q23: Which of the following is true for 'bilateral aid'?

a) It is given by the World Bank.
b) It may have to be spent with the donor country.
c) It is investment from multinational companies.
d) It is the reduction of trade barriers.

. . . .

Q24: Which one of the following groups contains an EU member, a Eurozone member, and a country **not** in the EU, in that order?

a) Spain, Ireland, Finland.
b) Sweden, Denmark, Switzerland.
c) UK, Poland, Cyprus.
d) Slovenia, Germany, Norway.

. . . .

Do not use bullet points to answer the following questions, as this usually leaves answers brief and undeveloped. Think in terms of 2 to 3 mark paragraphs. Make the basic point and then add an example or develop your first comment into something more complex. Move on to make another separate relevant point in a new paragraph.

Q25: Even before EU enlargement, the majority of UK trade was within the EU. If the UK were to join the eurozone, this would further strengthen its trade links with the EU.

Suggest reasons why the majority of UK trade is with the EU. *(SQA 2005)*

(5 marks)

....

Q26: What are the advantages and disadvantages for the UK of EU enlargement?

(10 marks)

....

Q27: Explain the main economic costs and benefits for the UK of joining the eurozone.

(10 marks)

....

Q28: Discuss how effective different types of aid are in increasing the growth rates of developing countries. *(SQA 2006)*

(12 Marks)

....

Q29: Discuss the view that "what developing countries need is free and fair trade, not aid". *(SQA 2006)*

(8 marks)

Note: one approach in answering this question would be to give the positive advantages of trade, and the negative side of aid. For balance, finish by pointing out that aid may sometimes be necessary.

....

....

Topic 6

End of unit test

End of Unit 3 test

Go online

Q1:   Match up the following nations with an appropriate description in the table below *(where there is more than one correct option, please choose the nation that is most suitable)*:

- Brazil;
- Canada;
- China;
- Japan;
- Malawi;
- Malta;
- Norway;
- USA.

Description	Nation
Major export market for UK	
Major source of UK imports	
Uses the yen as currency	
Uses the euro as currency	
Example of emerging economy	
Example of developing economy	
Example of developed economy	
European nation not in EU	

(10 marks)

. . . .

For the following questions, always attempt to extend and develop any initial point that you make. Think in terms of 2-mark paragraphs and support your assertions with evidence and/or examples. Economics can be a subtle subject and answers that explain the complex points well are generally well rewarded. Avoid bullet points - they will just encourage you to keep answers too brief and you will make unsupported assertions.

The solutions consists of paragraphs with mark allocations. You do not have to include all the points in your answer to gain full marks.

Q2:   Describe three trade barriers and explain the reasons governments may give to justify the imposition of trade barriers.

(10 marks)

. . . .

Q3: Explain possible economic effects on UK firms and consumers of the sterling exchange rate being high for a period of time?

(10 marks)

. . . .

Q4: Discuss the advantages and disadvantages for the UK economy of joining the euro.

(10 marks)

. . . .

Q5: Compare and contrast the main economic characteristics of developing countries with those of emerging countries.

(10 marks)

. . . .

. . . .

Glossary

Absolute advantage theory

a theory that shows numerically the gains from trade that occur when each of two nations produces the good it is more efficient at making

Balance of payments

an account recording the international transactions of UK residents. It consists of the current account, and the capital and financial account

Balance of trade

visible exports minus visible imports. The balance of trade refers only to trade in goods

Bilateral aid

aid from one country to another

Capital and financial account

includes transactions with the European Union and foreign direct investment

Clean (or pure) float

a floating exchange rate set entirely by the market without government intervention

Common Agricultural Policy (CAP)

an expensive system of subsidies paid to European Union farmers

Common external tariff

a tariff applying to the import of goods across the external border of the EU

Comparative advantage theory

a theory that shows numerically the gains from trade that occur when an advanced nation produces the good it has the greatest efficiency advantage in; the less advanced nation makes the good it has the least disadvantage in producing. Note that initially the advanced nation has an absolute advantage in producing both goods

Convergence

the need for an economy joining the single currency to match up with the economic indicators of existing eurozone members before joining

Current account

includes visibles (goods) and invisibles (services)

Deindustrialisation

loss of manufacturing capacity in a home country as manufacturing moves to lower cost locations abroad

Devaluation

a decrease in the value of a currency on the foreign exchange market. Under a fixed exchange rate system this would be announced as a step change. The term is also valid if applied to a decline in value in a floating system

Developed countries

advanced economies with high standards of living

Developing countries

the weakest economies with the lowest standards of living

Dirty float

the government (using its central bank) intervenes in the market to manipulate the exchange rate

Diversification

the term, in this topic, is applied to operating in more than one country - in diverse markets. This has the advantage that sales are unlikely to reduce in all markets at the same time

Economies of scale

advantages (mainly cost per unit reductions) that companies benefit from as they serve larger markets

Emerging economies

economies with high rates of foreign investment and economic growth, rapid industrialisation and increasing exports of manufactured goods

Enlargement

the widening of the European Union to include new members

Errors and omissions

this figure corrects any imbalance in the balance of payments. The double entry accounting system for recording international transactions means that the end figures on the balance of payments technically must always balance

Euro

the currency used by those EU members who have joined the eurozone

European Central Bank

the monetary authority for the eurozone

European Union

a free trade area of 28 countries (2014), including the UK

Eurozone

the name given to the group of EU countries that have adopted the euro as their currency

Exchange rate

the rate at which one currency can be changed for another

Exports

UK goods and services being sold outside the UK

Financial flows

international investment flows in and out of the UK

Fixed exchange rate

an agreed fixed rate for currency exchange set by governments

FOREX

an abbreviation of foreign exchange, the FOREX market is the market in which one currency can be exchange for another

Hot money

money that is moved quickly from one currency to another to take advantage of the best interest rates or in anticipation of making a profit from changing currency values

Human Development Index (HDI)

a system for measuring economic development by combining three factors - life expectancy, education levels and living standards

Imports

foreign goods and services being sold to the UK

Income flows

dividends and interest paid in and out of the UK

Infrastructure

a broad term usually referring to the economic framework provided by the transport and communication networks, the social facilities such as health, sanitation and education, or the legal system that enables business and government to operate effectively

Invisibles

refer to trade in services only

Multilateral aid

aid donated by international institutions such as the IMF or the World Bank

Multinational

a company that has production units based in foreign countries, rather than merely exporting from one base

The Pink Book

annual statistical publication on UK trade

Price transparency

comparisons of prices in different countries are made easier for consumers through the use of a single currency

Single market

a programme of policies adopted by the EU on 1 January 1993 which advanced beyond the mere abolition of trade barriers

Soft loans

loans given to developing or emerging economies at reduced interest rates

Standard of living

calculates the increased ability to purchase goods and services of the average consumer. It is used to define whether consumers are "better off" in material terms

Tied aid

aid from donor countries that requires developing economies to spend the money on goods supplied by the donor country

Trade deficit

imports of goods (or services) exceed exports of goods (or services)

Trade surplus

exports of goods (or services) exceed imports of goods (or services)

Transfers

payments to or from international institutions

Visibles

refer to trade in goods only

Answers to questions and activities

1 Understanding global trade

UK imports - EU countries (page 3)

Q1: The following 10 EU countries are highlighted below.

1.	**Germany (4)**	11.	Japan (5)
2.	China (23)	12.	**Sweden (15)**
3.	USA (1)	13.	Hong Kong (21)
4.	**Netherlands (8)**	14.	Switzerland (9)
5.	Norway (19)	15.	Russia (27)
6.	**France (2)**	16.	**Poland (20)**
7.	**Belgium/Luxembourg (11/17*)**	17.	Canada (16)
8.	**Italy (6)**	18.	**Denmark (21)**
9.	**Ireland (7)**	19.	India (10)
10.	**Spain (3)**	20.	Turkey (19)

UK trade by category (page 8)

Q2: a) True

Q3: b) False

Q4: a) True

Q5: b) False

Q6: b) False

The advantages of trade (page 10)

Q7: Trade allows countries to obtain products that they are unable to produce themselves. In the UK that will include fruits that cannot be grown easily because the climate is unsuitable.

Trade allows countries to obtain products from the cheapest, most efficient producers. This enables citizens to increase their standard of living as the money saved can be used to purchase more goods and services.

Trade creates increased competition, and companies with international markets can cut costs by increasing economies of scale. This benefits consumers through reduced prices and improved quality.

Impact of international trade (page 10)

Q8: a) Increase

Q9: a) Increase

Q10: b) Decrease

Q11: a) Increase

Q12: a) Increase

Globalisation (page 11)

Q13: Globalisation describes the rapid expansion of international *trade*. Some developments that have contributed are the reduction in the costs of transporting goods through the development of *containerisation* and the increasing ease of modern communications using the *internet*. These developments have led to multi-national firms reducing costs by finding new *locations* for production plants and the increasing prevalence of internationally recognised *brand* names.

Before-trade and after-trade output (absolute advantage) (page 14)

Q14: 90

Q15: 80

Q16: 100

Q17: 120

Q18: a) Yes

Before-trade and after-trade output (comparative advantage) (page 18)

Q19: a) True

Q20: b) False

Q21: a) True

Q22: a) True

Q23: a) True

Trade surplus or deficit (page 20)

Q24:

Trade in goods (2006)	Trade surplus	Trade deficit
USA	Yes	
Germany		Yes
China		Yes
India		Yes
Japan		Yes

Patterns and reasons for trends in trade (page 21)

Q25: a) neighbouring

Q26: b) more

Q27: a) large

Q28: a) more

Trading nations (page 22)

Q29: c) Germany

Q30: d) Morocco

Trading nations - Japan and Ireland (page 23)

Q31: a) Ireland

End of Topic 1 test (page 26)

Q32: *The marker will be expecting about 6 developed points, or a larger number of less developed points. Marks are attached to each scoring point in the model answer. The specimen answer actually has 14 scoring points - always best to take out some insurance if you want all the marks available. Note that there are many other points that could have been made, and if you remember and can quote some figures that would impress.*

Geographically, UK trade is focussed on the EU and the USA *(1 mark)*. The EU has grown in significance as more countries have joined *(1 mark)*. As a free trade area, trade occurs without barriers such as tariffs *(1 mark)*.

The UK remains a major producer of manufactured goods (e.g. cars) *(1 mark)*. The volume of oil exports is falling but with increases in the price of a barrel the value of oil exports could continue to rise *(1 mark)*. As there are different types and qualities of oil, we also need to import oil in similar quantities *(1 mark)*. The UK has a trade in goods deficit *(1 mark)*.

In contrast UK trade in services is in surplus *(1 mark)*. This is largely due to the UK's expertise in financial services and the eminence of London *(1 mark)* and, to a lesser extent, Edinburgh.

The impact of foreign direct investment has grown greatly in recent years *(1 mark)* with the UK near the top of the world league both as a source and a beneficiary of FDI *(1 mark)*.

Scottish exports include oil and gas (although this is attributed to the UK as a whole), whisky, financial services, oil and gas service industries, office machinery and tourism *(2 marks)*.

Q33: e) United Kingdom

Q34: d) Italy

Q35: b) China

Q36: a) Canada

Q37: c) Israel

Q38: f) Zambia

Q39: As a result of trade, consumers will have more **choice**, for example, **bananas**, that cannot be easily grown in the UK. Companies will face increased **competition** and as a result will have to increase **quality** and reduce **prices** to stay in business. This will mean that consumers will have a higher **standard** of **living**.

Q40: *Advice: This question is out of 8 marks only. Under exam conditions you should allow about 12 minutes for completion. Therefore a detailed explanation of absolute and comparative advantage using efficiency tables would be excessive. Try to explain the theories in words without tables. A simple approach would be to divide the question in two and attempt to gain 4 marks on each theory.*

The theory of absolute advantage uses an example of a two-country two-product world. Initially, before trade, both countries have to make both products, as they do not have the option of trading to obtain either item. When country A is more efficient at making product X and country B is more efficient at making product Y then trade will be beneficial. By specialising in the one product and trading, the after trade outcome is that more output is produced from the same inputs. This allows both countries to gain from trade, assuming that transport costs are low.

(Note that every sentence advances the explanation another step. This means that a marker is likely to tick each sentence, and award at last 4 marks.)

Comparative advantage takes the theory of absolute advantage further. It proves that even when country A is more efficient at making both products (X and Y) and country B is less efficient for both products, trade will still offer benefits. Country A with an absolute advantage in making both products should take on the production of the product it has the greatest advantage making when compared to country B. Country B will then specialise in the product in which has the least comparative disadvantage.

(Note that again every sentence moves the explanation along, and again the answer will accumulate ticks, and at least 4 marks.)

2 Multinationals

The countries in which BP operates (page 30)

Q1: At the time of writing the website has a tab for 'BP worldwide' where you will find details of their current operations around the planet. You could repeat this task for another firm of your choosing.

Location factors (page 30)

Q2: b) Infrastructure concerns

Q3: c) Risk factors

Q4: b) Infrastructure concerns

Q5: a) Cost factors

Q6: c) Risk factors

Q7: a) Cost factors

The effects on the host country (page 32)

Q8:

Positive	Negative
creates employment	may cause pollution
improves working conditions	may switch location
increases exports	only provides low skill jobs
introduces modern technology	profits often repatriated
trains workers	undercuts local firms' prices

The effects on the home country (page 33)

Q9:

Positive	Negative
profits repatriated	deindustrialisation
survival of home-based firm	fewer exports
	jobs are lost overseas

End of Topic 2 test (page 35)

Q10: d) First Group

Q11: b) produce in more than one country.

Q12: a) the repatriation of profits.

Q13: b) the repatriation of profits.

Q14: c) political instability.

Q15: For 6 marks you will need six of the following points, or a fewer number of points with development:

- wage rates;
- land prices;
- available labour force and its skills, including level of basic literacy;
- access to raw materials;
- the road, rail, sea and air links are sufficient to allow the firm to operate efficiently and without unpredictable delays in getting goods to the market;
- the country has access to the latest information and communications systems and these systems function adequately;
- there is a framework of business and contract law that facilitates business;
- the size of the local market - developing local markets is often crucial to success, and multinationals may withdraw from markets where they cannot reach a suitable level of customer demand and are consequently unable to deliver the economies of scale that lead to profit;
- there are trade barriers that will increase costs to consider;
- the chances of a violent revolution;
- the exchange rate of the currency changing;
- an epidemic or a natural disaster such as a flood.

3 Exchange rates

Demand for currency (page 40)

Q1: a) Increase

Q2: b) Decrease

Q3: a) Increase

Q4: a) Increase

The supply of currency (page 41)

Q5: The **supply of** sterling comes from the purchase of UK **imports** by **UK** consumers and companies.

Q6: It follows that **import penetration** helps to drive the value of a country's currency **downwards**, because it increases **supply of** that currency.

Q7: 'Hot money' flows are **taken out** of pounds whenever attractive interest rates are available **outside the UK**. **Decreases** in UK interest rates can lead to an **increased supply of** pounds, because of the **diminished** returns available in UK banks.

The effect of a rising exchange rate on the economy (page 42)

Q8: £72,000

Q9: £60,000

The effect of a rising exchange rate on inflation, economic growth and employment (page 44)

Q10: A rising exchange rate makes our exports more **expensive**, and our imports **cheaper**. This **increases** unemployment because UK goods are **less** price competitive in world markets. With less output economic growth **decreases**, and combined with a **negative** multiplier effect, there is a danger of **recession**.

The effect of a falling exchange rate (page 44)

Q11: A falling exchange rate for the pound will make our **exports** cheaper and our **imports** more expensive. This will make UK exporters **more** price competitive. In the UK market foreign firms will be under pressure to **raise** prices. As a result UK firms may increase sales and output thus increasing economic **growth**. This will create more **employment** in the UK. However the cost of imports will make **inflation** higher.

Fixed exchange rates (page 46)

Q12: Fixed exchange rates allow firms to trade with *certainty* that exchange rate movements will not affect the *profitability* of international contracts. For long periods, *speculation* will not take place because *central* banks will successfully maintain the currency value.

Floating exchange rates (page 48)

Q13: Floating exchange rates *automatically* adjust to prevailing economic conditions. No *intervention* by central banks means that large *reserves* of foreign currency are not required and *speculators* find it difficult to spot an inappropriate exchange value to *profit* from when the rates reflect prevailing economic conditions.

Exchange rate systems (page 48)

Q14: a) Advantage for fixed exchange rate

Q15: b) Advantage for floating exchange rate

Q16: b) Advantage for floating exchange rate

Q17: a) Advantage for fixed exchange rate

Trends in the pound to dollar exchange rate (page 50)

Q18:

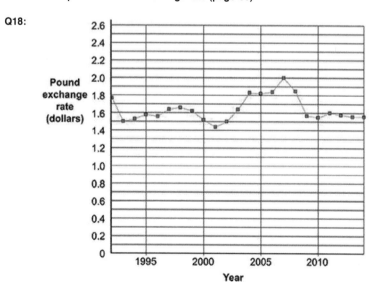

End of Topic 3 test (page 52)

Q19: a) exports from the UK increase.

Q20: d) increase exports.

Q21: a) as economies grow at different rates, they become unsustainable.

Q22: d) interest rates.

Q23: c) Both of the above.

Q24: You should provide an explanation of how the demand for sterling is determined by:

- the demand for UK exports;
- the level of FDI in the UK;
- the amount of tourists visiting the UK;
- hot money inflows.

(1 mark for each determinant and 1 mark for each explanation)

Full marks can also be gained for explaining the factors which influence the determinants, e.g. relative inflation rates, the UK rate of interest, and the state of the UK economy.

Q25: *"Discuss" means discuss points in favour and points against. Some points made here can be quite complex and if well discussed and might be worthy of 3 marks. Try to explain at least two advantages and two disadvantages to target full marks.*

The advantages include:

- no need to defend a particular exchange rate;
- can adopt an independent monetary policy;
- possible automatic adjustment to the Balance of Payments (Marshall Lerner).

(Maximum 6 marks)

The disadvantages include:

- fluctuating exchange rates - therefore trade becomes more risky;
- greater risk of high inflation;
- can lead to a depreciation/inflation spiral;
- greater scope for currency arbitrage.

(Maximum 6 marks)

Q26: *This answer to this question can extend beyond the current section. However you can start by developing the first part of your answer along the lines of how a fall in interest rates reduces the exchange value of sterling and go on to explain how this can impact on inflation through rising import prices.*

The main problem is the risk of overheating with the consequent rise in demand-pull inflation, trade deficits - so look for a detailed explanation of why AMD will rise, e.g. borrowing cheaper, saving less rewarding, marginal investments now viable, and increased real income of mortgage holders.

This is all that is required for full marks but other reasons include the fall in the value of sterling because of hot money outflows leading to an increase in the price of imports and cost-push prices, a large increase in house prices (because of cheaper mortgages) and an increase in consumer debt.

(Maximum of 2 marks each)

4 The balance of payments

Visible or invisible (page 58)

Q1: a) Visible

Q2: b) Invisible

Q3: b) Invisible

Q4: a) Visible

Visibles (page 59)

Q5:

Year	Export of goods (£ billion)	Import of goods (£ billion)	Visible balance (£ billion)
2010	271	368	-97
2011	309	406	-97
2012	305	414	-109
2013	307	419	-112
2014	292	412	-120

Q6:

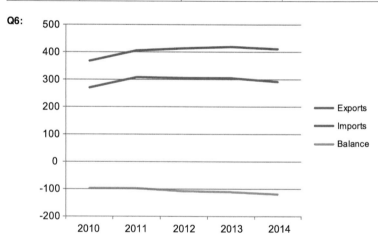

Invisibles (page 59)

Q7:

Year	Export of services (£ billion)	Import of services (£ billion)	Invisible balance (£ billion)
2010	176	116	60
2011	190	118	72
2012	196	121	75
2013	209	130	79
2014	208	123	85

Q8:

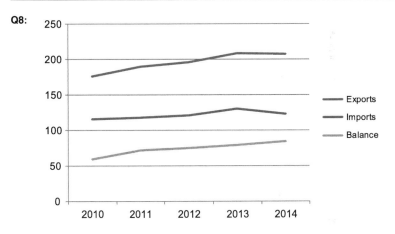

Surpluses and deficits (page 61)

Q9: The UK has a *deficit* in trade in goods, but a smaller *surplus* in trade in services. Taken together the overall UK *current* account is in deficit. Two factors causing this are low *wages* overseas and a £ exchange rate that for periods can be *high*. Fortunately the UK enjoys net *capital* inflows and has a strong *financial services* sector based around the pre-eminence of *London*.

Costs and benefits of foreign direct investment (page 63)

Q10: Your answer could develop several of the following points:

- jobs are created by the investment in construction and then in operations;
- the multiplier effect further increases the employment effects in the local community;
- the jobs are often on the assembly line with few higher paid posts for locals;

- multinationals show little loyalty in recessions and branch plants often close first;
- multinationals are footloose and may move on after a few years to a cheaper location;
- management skills from abroad are introduced;
- the investment counts towards the balance of payments as a credit;
- the multinational will be keen to export from Scotland to the EU improving the trade balance;
- wages and working conditions may be more attractive in these multinationals and local firms face higher costs to match them, or struggle to find staff;
- the tax base for local authorities in Scotland will increase and this provides funds for local authority services.

Trends in the current account (page 64)

Q11: Combined, the trade in goods and services have moved from a small surplus in 1997 to a significant deficit of between £30bn and £40bn in recent years to 2013.

Q12: The current account balance has moved into greater deficit since 1998, from less than £5bn to more than £70bn in 2013. As a percentage of GDP it has moved from less than 1% in 1998 to more than 4% in 2013.

Trends in the trade in goods and services (page 65)

Q13: The trade in services surplus has increased from less than £20bn before 2003 upwards to a surplus of nearly £80bn in 2013. The trade in goods deficit has widened from less than £20bn in 1997 to £110bn in 2013.

End of Topic 4 test (page 67)

Q14: c) trade in services.

Q15: c) show a deficit for goods and a surplus for services.

Q16: c) Both of the above.

Q17: c) foreign direct investment.

Q18: a) visibles and invisibles.

Q19: *The development of the answer with examples is probably not essential with only 4 marks at stake. However it is included because you will not be sure what the markers' instructions are, so it is safer to add some relevant details or examples to most answers.*

A trade in goods deficit means that exports of goods (e.g. tangible items such as cars) are less than imports of goods. The UK has a substantial deficit in goods.

A budget deficit describes the government spending more (e.g. on the NHS) than it takes in through tax revenue (e.g. income tax) in a year. The government has to borrow to make up for the shortfall.

Q20: Budget deficits speed up the economy. The government is putting more money in as government spending than it is taking out in taxes. This will lead to decreased unemployment. Companies receiving government contracts will have to hire more staff. The government will also directly employ more teachers, doctors, etc. in the public sector. When the newly employed spend their incomes there will be a multiplier effect and a new round of jobs created.

When the UK economy grows fast, the demand for goods and services begins to exceed the supply. Especially as full employment is reached, increases in supply become difficult to achieve. As a result more and more imports are sucked in to satisfy the demand from UK consumers. Imports will exceed exports. Thus a budget deficit leads to a trade deficit.

Q21: At times the exchange rate of the pound sterling has been relatively high against the currencies of our major trading partners. This makes our exports less price competitive in foreign markets, and at home imports will be cheaper. Sales of foreign goods increase as they are substituted for the higher priced UK goods. This led to a growing trade deficit.

Labour costs in much of the world are cheaper than in the UK. The rapidly growing economies such as those of Eastern Europe and of China are producing more and more manufactured goods. These goods are priced at less than those made in the UK, so UK firms are losing customers in home and foreign markets. For example, shoe manufacturing in the UK has declined in the face of cheap imports. This leads to a growing trade in goods deficit.

5 Understanding the impact of the global economy

The eurozone (page 71)

Q1: Eurozone countries

Austria	Belgium	Cyprus	Estonia
Finland	France	Germany	Greece
Ireland	Italy	Latvia	Lithuania
Luxembourg	Malta	Netherlands	Portugal
Slovakia	Slovenia	Spain	

Joining the euro - advantages and disadvantages for the UK (page 73)

Q2:

Advantages of joining the euro	Disadvantages of joining the euro
Easier for consumers to compare prices in different countries	One interest rate set for all of eurozone
No commission on changing currency	Devaluation of pound no longer possible
Exchange rate certainty for firms within eurozone	
Multinational investment in UK more likely	

Enlargement of the EU - benefits and problems for the UK (page 76)

Q3:

Benefits of enlargement for the UK	Problems of enlargement for the UK
Wider markets for UK goods	Additional EU budget costs for the UK
Increased choice for UK consumers	Multinationals move to cheaper locations
Skilled workers from abroad to fill vacancies	

Human Development Index (HDI) of the countries of the world (page 77)

Expected answer

You will find many of the highest ranked countries in Europe and North America. Parts of Africa will feature among the lowest ranked countries.

Levels of development (page 77)

Q4:

Nation	Income per person ($)	Life Expectancy (years)	Literacy Rate (%)	Developing/ Emerging/ Developed
Malawi	900	60	75	Developing
India	4,000	68	63	Emerging
Bangladesh	2,100	71	58	Developing
Japan	37,100	84	99	Developed
South Africa	11,500	50	93	Emerging
Sweden	40,900	82	99	Developed
Chad	2,500	49	35	Developing
United Kingdom	37,300	80	99	Developed
Brazil	12,100	73	90	Emerging

Note: The answers are not always clear-cut. For example, South Africa has a life expectancy more in keeping with a developing country than an emerging country.

World Factbook (page 78)

Expected answer

There is no definitive solution to this task - it depends on your choice of countries.

Developing countries (page 79)

Q5:

Land	Labour	Capital
Droughts leading to crop failure	Low literacy rates	Lack of modern technology
Few natural resources	Poor health	Little is saved
Seasonal flooding	Unskilled workers	Poor transport infrastructure
		Weak banking system

Senegal (page 82)

Q6: b) 61

Q7: a) 50%

Q8: b) $2,100

Q9: c) 54%

Q10: c) 78%

Q11: b) 43%

Aid versus trade (page 84)

Q12:

Type of aid	Description	Problem
Bilateral aid	From one country to another	Tied to buying from donor country
Multilateral aid	From international organisation	Economic "strings" attached (e.g. balanced budget)
Emergency aid	Disaster relief (food and medicine)	May encourage dependency
Soft loans	Low interest finance to assist development	Increases debts

Emerging economies (page 85)

Q13: Emerging economies such as *Brazil* no longer depend on *primary* production. They tend to have *high* levels of spending on infrastructure. Literacy rates are *over* 50% as a result of these spending levels on education. *High* levels of foreign investment occur, encouraged by political *stability*. GDP per capita, for example, could be *$10,000* per annum and standards of living are *rising*. With *increasing* levels of birth control, the age structure of emerging economies shows more people in the *working* age categories.

Malaysia (page 87)

Q14: b) 75

Q15: c) 93%

Q16: b) $17,500

Q17: a) 4%

Q18: a) 11%

Q19: c) 29%

End of topic test (page 90)

Q20: b) monetary policy.

Q21: b) Malawi, India, Japan.

Q22: c) Free trade with EU members.

Q23: b) It may have to be spent with the donor country.

Q24: d) Slovenia, Germany, Norway.

Q25: The UK trades mainly with the EU because there are no trade barriers such as tariffs between EU countries. This means that the prices of traded goods are not subject to taxes as they cross frontiers and can compete fairly in foreign markets.

The EU has a large population and is a single market of over 400 million consumers. Paperwork and frontier delays have been reduced making it easier to export and import.

The EU consumers have high incomes and spend a lot on goods and services. They are also close to the UK so that transport costs on goods are less, and share a similar culture and tastes. This makes exporting to them more likely to be successful.

Q26: *Advantages*

Shortages in the labour market will be filled by immigrants from the new members seeking the higher wages of the UK. This will benefit firms who would have production problems if they could not find the appropriate applicants among UK citizens.

Wage inflation that would result from skill shortages will be far less likely to occur. Employers will no longer have to attract workers from other firms by outbidding them on wages. This will help the UK economy to meet its 2% inflation target.

Enlargement provides a bigger single market for UK firms and they may increase economies of scale. Faced with more competition they will need to be more innovative and to hold down prices for consumers.

Disadvantages

The low-wage new members may attract multi-nationals to invest away from the UK, creating unemployment. Low priced imports may attract consumers away from UK produced goods and this will reduce profits and dividends, and increase unemployment.

The new members will be eligible for EU funds to develop their economies and support their farmers. The UK will be a net contributor to this growing bill.

Q27: Economic costs to the UK would include the large initial expense of changing all the coins and notes, and the changes required to slot machines.

If the UK joined the euro then the option of devaluing our currency would be lost from our economic policy options. If the economy suffered from low productivity or our exports were difficult to price competitively because of UK inflation it would no longer be possible to boost the economy through devaluation.

The interest rate set by the European Central Bank for the eurozone may not always be appropriate to the needs of the UK. If the UK is moving into recession it may benefit from lower interest rates but cannot be sure that the ECB will lower the eurozone interest rate. The UK economy might move into recession as a direct result of this. The UK would lose control of monetary policy, although it would keep some influence on the eurozone rate.

Benefits include the greater certainty for companies that they will not lose profit because of adverse exchange rate movements. Foreign direct investment in the UK may increase because of this, creating jobs.

The absence of currency conversion costs will also attract them as costs are lowered.

Q28: *Note the use of "discuss" which means that both positive and negative aspects of aid must be dealt with. If you are able to develop 4 points thoroughly you may well be awarded all 12 marks. Another approach is to provide 6 points and develop them to an extent.*

Solution: Here are a selection of points that you could discuss in your answer, they are in note form. You would need to develop them in your answer.

Type of aid: emergency relief - e.g food aid. Positive effect: saves lives. Negative effect: risk of dependency, undercuts local farmers.

Type of aid: infrastructure projects - e.g. dams. Positive effect: generally advantageous, e.g. increased crop yield. Negative effect: not good for communities cleared to make way.

Type of aid: providing university education in developed countries. Positive effect: graduates return with skills to assist progress. Negative effect: some may remain abroad, but generally positive.

Type of aid: "soft loans" - made at below commercial interest rates. Positive effect: used for investment in infrastructure. Negative effect: corruption may siphon off money from intended use.

Type of aid: tied aid - i.e. buy from donor country. Positive effect: receive equipment as a result of tied aid. Negative effect: no choice - may not get best value or most suitable.

Type of aid: multilateral aid - e.g. from World Bank. Positive effect: funds to develop economic infrastructure. Negative effect: expected to find market solutions, curb public spending.

Q29: *This specimen answer indicates some scoring points - 18 marks in all. Don't be put off by this. You can obtain the full 8 marks from a less detailed response. Remember that "discuss" requires you to consider the pros and cons.*

Allowing LDCs access to markets such as the EU's without facing tariff barriers and unfairly subsidised EU food will lead to greater orders for farmers in the LDC *(1 mark)*. As cheap producers they have a comparative advantage in the production of some primary products *(1 mark)*. Free trade will lead to higher revenues, more employment, better wages and investment in agriculture *(2 marks)*. This will have positive multiplier effects on all other sectors of the economy *(1 mark)*. Economic growth will increase *(1 mark)*. This will develop the ability of the LDC to sustain itself without aid *(1 mark)*. It will contribute export revenues to help the trade balance *(1 mark)*. It will increase the government's tax revenues *(1 mark)* and they can be invested in infrastructure such as health, education and transport *(1 mark)*.

Aid can only provide temporary relief *(1 mark)*. It may encourage dependency *(1 mark)* as it is difficult for local enterprise to compete with free hand-outs *(1 mark)*. If you cannot make a profit you may not plant the seed *(1 mark)*.

However, aid is valuable in times of flood or drought *(1 mark)*. It keeps people alive, at least in the short term *(1 mark)*. Grants for infrastructure projects (e.g. water and sanitation) can also help to develop the economy *(1 mark)*. Both aid and trade can be helpful, but the long-term solution may come from free trade *(1 mark)*.

6 End of unit test

End of Unit 3 test (page 94)

Q1:

Description	Nation
Major export market for UK	USA
Major source of UK imports	China
Uses the yen as currency	Japan
Uses the euro as currency	Malta
Example of emerging economy	Brazil
Example of developing economy	Malawi
Example of developed economy	Canada
European nation not in EU	Norway

Note: It is also true that the USA is a significant source of UK imports. However, none of the other examples are in the top export markets. USA should therefore be the choice for the major export market for UK.

Q2: *Trade barriers (6 marks)*

Any three of the following trade barriers - worth 2 marks each. Always give examples if you can, they can help you to get the full marks if your description is weak.

A quota is a limit by value or volume on imports. There are many examples of quotas around the world. In the past the EU has placed a limit on the import of textiles from China. *(2 marks)*

An embargo is a total ban on imports, perhaps because of political or military conflict. It can also happen for health reasons so British beef was subject to an embargo when BSE affected the herd. American beef is also the subject of embargoes because of their use of growth hormones in the feed. *(2 marks)*

A tariff is a tax on imports that increases the price of the import and therefore reduces sales and advantages home produced goods. For example Scotch whisky faces high tariffs in many markets e.g. India. In 2006 imported leather shoes from China were subjected to a 19% tariff entering the EU. *(2 marks)*

A subsidy is assistance that gives home producers a cost advantage over imports. This government financial help can take many forms, but essentially allows a less efficient home-based company to charge less and continue competing against efficient importers. The Common Agricultural Policy of the EU is an excellent example of subsidies to home producers enabling them to compete with cheap imports. *(2 marks)*

An administrative delay is an artificially created bureaucratic (paperwork) hold-up, that adds to the importer's costs. Any delay in getting goods on the shelf adds to costs, and there is always the chance that importers may look to find easier opportunities in other countries. *(2 marks)*

Justifications *(4 marks)*

Any two of the following justifications - worth 2 marks each.

Avoiding job losses - imports take custom away from home producers of the same good or service. This would lead to job losses, that may be concentrated in one region with negative multiplier effects. *(2 marks)*

The Infant Industry Argument is a strong one when properly applied. It protects a new industry's home market until it is large enough to enjoy economies of scale and compete freely on world markets. *(2 marks)*

Retaliation is a reaction to unfair trade by another country. For example "dumping" items below cost price may lead to tariffs as retaliation. *(2 marks)*

Trade deficits can be corrected by reducing imports. This assumes that there is no retaliation against the country imposing the initial trade barrier. *(2 marks)*

Q3: UK firms:

Exporting firms will find it difficult to compete in foreign markets. The high exchange rate forces them to increase prices abroad or accept a substantial cut in profit margins. *(2 marks)*

Example: a Jaguar car selling for £30,000 in the UK will at £1 = $2 be priced at $60,000 in the USA. If the pound gets stronger (£1 = $2.50) then the price in dollars would be $75,000. *(2 marks)*

This price rise will cause demand to fall, and when fewer are sold, then profits will fall. Alternatively they need to increase productivity and lower their average costs so that they can regain competitive prices. *(2 marks)*

Goods imported into the UK will be cheaper. This will increase price competition for import-competing UK firms. Sales and profits will be reduced. Some may go bankrupt. Alternatively they need to increase productivity and lower their average costs so they can be competitive on price once more. *(3 marks)*

Firms that use imported raw materials and components will gain from cheaper input prices. They still face stiffer price competition with foreign firms as a result of the higher exchange rate, but at least a reduction in some of their costs will help. *(2 marks)*

In summary UK firms will need to increase productivity to compensate for the loss of competitiveness. They could also seek to differentiate their products so that they have fewer substitutes and have lower price elasticity. *(2 marks)*

UK consumers:

If you are consuming a holiday abroad the strong pound will make it cheaper. If your hotel was going to charge you $900, then at £1= $2, this would be £450. If the pound strengthens to $3 and buys more dollars then your hotel may only charge you £300. *(2 marks)*

Imported products will be cheaper. Home-based firms may lower prices to be competitive. Inflation is reduced and your salary will buy more goods and services - an increase in your standard of living. *(3 marks)*

Q4: Advantages:

Joining the euro increases price transparency for UK consumers, allowing prices to be compared without exchange rate fluctuations clouding the issue. *(2 marks)*

Currency conversion costs for UK firms and consumers are eliminated when dealing with other eurozone countries. This may make the UK more attractive for foreign investment as multinationals can locate in the UK and export to the eurozone at lower cost. Costs for import/export are reduced and therefore prices should fall. This increase the standard of living as a price cut has the same effect as a pay rise. *(4 marks)*

There is certainty for businesses dealing with the eurozone that adverse currency fluctuations will not reduce their profits. This may attract multinationals to set up in the UK (foreign direct investment) and use it as a base for exporting to the eurozone. *(2 marks)*

There is an argument that the European Central Bank will take a strong line on controlling inflation, although the Bank of England has been given independence to do the same so this argument is now weaker. *(1 mark)*

Disadvantages:

One currency means one interest rate. The euro interest rate is set for the entire eurozone. It may not suit the needs of the UK economy if we are not at the same point in the business cycle as other euro economies. We may want a high rate to slow inflation and they may need a low rate to cure unemployment. *(3 marks)*

The UK can no longer set an independent economic policy. With limited influence over interest rates, the government will need to use fiscal policy to adjust the economy. The ability to devalue or depreciate the currency to solve a balance of payments deficit is also lost. It would now be necessary to have a budget surplus and squeeze the economy with higher taxes and cuts in government spending in order to cut imports. *(4 marks)*

Q5: *A "compare and contrast" question needs careful handling. You should compare points alongside each other. This solution consists of paragraphs with mark allocations. You do not have to include all the points in your answer.*

Developing countries have lower GDP per capita than emerging economies. They are far poorer. Typically a developing country like Malawi may have $800 per annum average income, but an emerging economy may have $5,000 or more per annum average income. *(2 marks)*

As a result a developing country's poverty leads to lower life expectancies and poorer health. This impacts on the ability of developing countries to produce at the same level as emerging economies. *(2 marks)*

Both developing countries and emerging economies tend to have international debts. However emerging economies have greater ability to pay the interest on the debt. Emerging economies borrow to invest in infrastructure projects such as roads and harbours that help to attract multinational investment. Developing countries are more likely to use the loans for crisis management in their struggling health and education services, or to pay for clean water projects or just for imported oil. *(3 marks)*

Developing countries have a higher percentage of the population employed in primary production, especially agriculture. Emerging economies have a more diverse employment profile with far more people employed in factories and services in their growing urbanisation. *(2 marks)*

Developing countries may rely heavily on the world price of one major export, often a crop. Emerging economies export a range of manufactured goods as well as crops. *(2 marks)*

Emerging economies have high rates of economic growth (e.g. China, Brazil, India). Rates of 8% growth and more have been known. However developing countries can struggle to make any growth - their agricultural economies can be hit by flood and drought. Developing countries do not produce a surplus to invest in the future. This limits their growth as does a weak banking system. *(4 marks)*

Developing countries tend to be more politically unstable than emerging economies and this does not make them safe for foreign investors. Military spending can be high relative to the economy, and corruption has a bigger impact on developing countries. Emerging economies flourish under strong leadership with an enterprise bias and democratically elected governments, e.g. Singapore. *(2 marks)*